W9-CTH-655

NEW DIRECTIONS FOR COMMUNITY COLLEGES

Arthur M. Cohen
EDITOR-IN-CHIEF

Florence B. Brawer
ASSOCIATE EDITOR

The Role of the Learning Resources Center in Instruction

Margaret Holleman
Pima Community College, Tucson, Arizona

EDITOR

Number 71, Fall 1990

JOSSEY-BASS INC., PUBLISHERS
San Francisco

THE ROLE OF THE LEARNING RESOURCES CENTER IN INSTRUCTION
Margaret Holleman (ed.)
New Directions for Community Colleges, no. 71
Volume XVIII, number 3
Arthur M. Cohen, Editor-in-Chief
Florence B. Brawer, Associate Editor

Microfilm copies of issues and articles are available in 16mm and 35mm, as well as microfiche in 105mm, through University Microfilms Inc., 300 North Zeeb Road, Ann Arbor, Michigan 48106.

LC 85-644753   ISSN 0194-3081   ISBN 1-55542-803-7

NEW DIRECTIONS FOR COMMUNITY COLLEGES is part of The Jossey-Bass Higher and Adult Education Series and is published quarterly by Jossey-Bass Inc., Publishers (publication number USPS 121-710) in association with the ERIC Clearinghouse for Junior Colleges. Second-class postage paid at San Francisco, California, and at additional mailing offices. Postmaster: Send address changes to Jossey-Bass Inc., Publishers, 350 Sansome Street, San Francisco, California 94104.

THE MATERIAL in this publication is based on work sponsored wholly or in part by the Office of Educational Research and Improvement, U.S. Department of Education, under contract number RI-88-062002. Its contents do not necessarily reflect the views of the Department, or any other agency of the U.S. Government.

EDITORIAL CORRESPONDENCE should be sent to the Editor-in-Chief, Arthur M. Cohen, at the ERIC Clearinghouse for Junior Colleges, University of California, Los Angeles, California 90024.

Cover photograph by Rene Sheret, Los Angeles, California © 1990.

Printed on acid-free paper in the United States of America.

Contents

034370

EDITOR'S NOTES

Fifty years ago, B. Lamar Johnson (1939) described a Carnegie Corporation-supported experiment, in a two-year college, which proved to be the forerunner of the modern learning resources center (LRC). In his combined capacity of college librarian and dean of instruction at Stephens College (Missouri), Johnson made the library central to the college's instructional program by broadening the concept of library materials and involving librarians in classroom teaching and professional development programs. Almost fifty years later, another Carnegie-supported study (Boyer, 1987) made similar recommendations for revitalizing undergraduate libraries, urging them to make connections—often through new technology—with the curriculum, classroom, faculty, and community at large.

The concept of the modern LRC, as described in the professional standards and used in this volume, is that of a configuration of various resource units that provides a systems approach to supporting the college's mission and instructional program. Such a configuration may include libraries; audiovisual centers; media-production and equipment-distribution units; testing centers; learning, tutoring, language, and microcomputer labs; staff development centers; instructional design and development services; print and copy shops; and radio or television stations, whether centrally administered or not. Bock (1984, p. 43) notes that debate over whether "libraries were solely support services or were instructional units was resolved in the '70s . . . when the LRCs became vital components of a heuristic approach to learning . . . utilizing both people and media in individualized small- and large-group instruction."

Recent Trends Affecting Community College LRCs

The role of the LRC in instruction is evolving in response to the following interrelated influences:

National and State Efforts at Educational Reform. Community colleges are expected to maintain educational excellence while retaining the open-door policies that have offered expanded opportunities to mushrooming enrollments of nontraditional students, many of whom—as a result of state-mandated assessment testing—will require remedial classes and other special assistance to become eligible for regular programs. The nation's business community, regional accrediting commissions, numerous books and articles (Breivik, 1987; Finn, 1989; Boyer, 1987; Hirsch, 1987), and several widely publicized studies (such as *Alliance for Excellence,* and the American Association of Community and Junior Colleges' *Building Communities*) have called for other changes in the college. These include incorporating a core of common learning; providing instruction in basic skills, including information, microcomputer, and global literacy; and training students to engage in the types of analytical thinking and problem solving that will make them independent, lifelong learners in our "information society."

Rapid Technological Developments. New technology has enhanced classroom instruction and permitted colleges to provide increasingly sophisticated types of alternative instructional delivery systems for nontraditional and off-campus students. Improved telecommunications systems have also dramatically expanded access to information for faculty and students.

Organization of This Volume

The developments just described have prompted LRC professionals to make the kinds of necessary connections that Boyer (1987) recommends. The first five chapters of this volume describe the involvement of LRC staff in curriculum change. LRC staff are joining faculty in designing integrated assignments (especially for writing and developmental education classes) to teach basic skills and critical thinking. They are also working with faculty to internationalize the curriculum and enhance professional development programs. The next four chapters describe some programs that LRC staff have initiated in response to recent trends. Staff are using learning theory to design telecourses and other types of distance education and to integrate microcomputers and experiential learning activities into classes. They are also using new technology to provide high-quality LRC support for off-campus courses. The final three chapters describe how an LRC can evaluate its role in instruction—in response to mandated program assessment, accrediting criteria, and professional standards—in order to plan for the future. In summary, the chapters in this volume reflect the work that community college LRC staff have been engaged in to "build communities," work on interdisciplinary instructional teams, and become involved in all types of literacy efforts (basic, informational, global, microcomputer, cultural, and civic) for all types of patrons.

Margaret Mead (1974) has described the community college as a "center for community action . . . that takes in four generations . . . with retired admirals who have never had a chance to study philosophy sitting next to sixteen-year-old kids and relating to each other . . . bringing back women who have been in households—together [with] day care centers on the premises . . . making the community college into a kind of microcosm of an acting, interrelating community group." For Mead, however, a community must have a soul: "A town that has no university and no museum, no theater, no art gallery . . . has no focus of lively interaction and interest in the people . . . just doesn't have a goal." Mead could well have included libraries in that list, for the LRC can serve as that type of catalyst in the community college.

Marianne Ryan and Isabel Leroy have helped the LRC at South Mountain Community College (Phoenix, Arizona) become such a catalyst. The college is in an area of the city without good public library and transportation services, where the population is one-third Hispanic, one-third Anglo, and one-third African-American, and where few youth complete junior high school. Their outreach program "combines the ideals and goals of the community college philosophy with the educational style and techniques of libraries" ("Leroy and Ryan," 1989). For the past three years, South Mountain's LRC has been sponsoring activities that have won the support of community agencies, civic and service organizations, and church groups and that have involved the neighborhood's parents and children in college-sponsored story hours, reading programs, crafts lessons, library tours, museum field trips, Saturday youth programs, and summer computer camps. According to Ryan (personal communication, 1989), the purpose of the program is to create a loving, exciting environment that builds self-esteem and encourages lifelong learning, making the college and the LRC appealing, comfortable, and familiar to both adults and at-risk students. Although this outreach program is probably unique in the nation, it epitomizes the potential for LRCs to make vital connections and build the types of communities crucial to the community college's mission and instructional program.

Margaret Holleman
Editor

References

Alliance for Excellence: Librarians Respond to A Nation at Risk. Washington, D.C.: U.S. Department of Education, 1984. 71 pp. (ED 243 885)

American Association of Community and Junior Colleges. *Building Communities: A Vision for a New Century.* Washington, D.C.: American Association of Community and Junior Colleges, 1988. 58 pp. (ED 293 578)

Bock, D. J. "From Libraries to Learning Resources: Six Decades of Progress—and Still Changing." *Community & Junior College Libraries,* 1984, 3 (2), 35–46.

Boyer, E. L. *College: The Undergraduate Experience in America.* New York: Harper & Row, 1987.

Breivik, P. S. "Making the Most of Libraries." *Change,* 1987, 19 (4), 44–52.

Finn, C. E. "Community Colleges Should Embrace a Common Core of Learning." *Community College Week,* Jan. 2, 1989, pp. 5–6.

Hirsch, E. D., Jr. *Cultural Literacy: What Every American Needs to Know.* Boston: Houghton Mifflin, 1987.

Johnson, B. L. *Vitalizing a College Library.* Chicago: American Library Association, 1939.

"Leroy and Ryan Selected 1988 Innovators of the Year." *Arizona State Library Association Newsletter,* 1989, 22 (2), 1, 3.

Mead, M. Presentation Before the Washington, D.C., Anthropological Society, May 21, 1974.

Margaret Holleman is director of library services at the West Campus of Pima Community College, Tucson, Arizona. She has been editor of the quarterly Community & Junior College Libraries *since its inception in 1982.*

*Relationships between library research and critical-thinking skills
are related to goals in student assessment. When teams of librarians
and faculty develop assignments that require students to use library
resources, learning is strengthened and enriched.*

Linking the LRC
with Student Assessment

Gloria Terwilliger

The quality of American education is under intensive scrutiny. Initially, the
focus was on primary and secondary schools, a focus fostered by public
concern about the ability of high school graduates to function effectively in
an increasingly complex technological economy. Pressure on colleges and
universities to respond to the same questions about the quality of learning
and teaching has escalated over the last few years, since Finn's (1984)
indictment of higher education. Finn's predictions were closely followed
by the action he described: "It is only a matter of time before citizens'
groups, business task forces, governors, legislative leaders, congressional
committee chairmen, editorial writers, the mainstream foundations, and
miscellaneous critics, pundits, and savants begin to make a huge ruckus
over the standards and performance of colleges and universities" (Finn,
1984, p. 29).

A Brief Review of Student Assessment

The focus did indeed shift to the colleges and universities, its intensity
fueled by declining scores on national assessment tests and SATs, grave
warnings about "a nation at risk," criticisms of the decline of liberal arts
education and the "closing of the American mind," and laments over the
lack of general "cultural literacy." Citizens have been appalled by the results
of national knowledge surveys, which reveal gaps in traditional "common
knowledge" among college graduates, and there is growing concern over
difficulties in achieving clarity of communication in our multicultural
nation.

NEW DIRECTIONS FOR COMMUNITY COLLEGES, no. 71, Fall 1990 © Jossey-Bass Inc., Publishers

"What do students learn?" is a question being asked by the groups that Finn named, as well as by citizens at all levels of society. Irrevocably linked to this question is the cost of running the educational institution. Moreover, the economic issue is not limited to the public sector. Governing boards of private institutions are equally dismayed by negative reports on the state of American education, by expanding educational costs, and by their own dependence on the corporate zeal of college development offices.

The question of what is learned for the amount invested reflects the two aspects of assessment: instructional improvement and institutional accountability. This question probes the fundamental functions of education in any society: to ensure the transmission of knowledge, and to provide effective professionals, technicians, skilled workers, and qualified leaders to ensure the future of the nation. The academic community has been forced to move out of the virtually inviolate position of monitoring itself, and into the unwelcome, often uncomfortable, visibility of public review.

Assessment Methodology. The complexity of carrying out an assessment of higher education in this country is mirrored by the variety of initiatives, projects, and procedures. The process varies from state to state, and methodology varies considerably within similar activities. The most consistent trend has reflected the general tendency to focus more on institutional accountability than on instructional improvement. Peter Ewell, savant of assessment, has described the variety of the content of institutional assessment programs as including "anything from standardized testing of basic skills to in-depth investigations of such elusive qualities as critical thinking and problem solving" (Ewell, 1987a, p. 24).

Assessment of educational outcomes is becoming formalized as more and more states introduce legislation that mandates it. In all but a few instances, however, state authorities have given institutions the latitude to devise and implement assessment plans that fit their own curricula and students. Ewell (1987b) points out four basic kinds of outcomes that determine the diversity of assessment efforts: outcomes concerning knowledge, skills, attitudes and values, and behavior. He divides the skills dimension into basic skills, cognitive skills, knowledge-building skills, and the types of skills required for licensing in particular occupations or professions.

Assessment Methodology and the Teaching Role of the Library. Ewell's (1987b) descriptions of the cognitive and knowledge-building skills are particularly important in identifying the role of libraries in the assessment process: "The second skills area consists of such higher-order cognitive skills as critical thinking, problem solving, and other complex applications of information and learned techniques. . . . Because they are complex, however, available testing instruments are scarce, and such skills are seldom directly assessed outside individual classrooms. Equally important, though seldom explicitly identified as part of college outcomes, is the third area, knowledge-building skills, including skills associated with locating existing knowledge through library catalogues, computer archives, and other sources" (Ewell, 1987b, p. 14).

The significance of the library in the educational process has been noted by Ernest Boyer of the Carnegie Commission, who emphasizes the self-directed learning that can occur through informed use of the library, learning "in which students become increasingly independent, increasingly creative, and increasingly [able to] link knowledge across the disciplines" (cited in Breivik, 1987, p. 45).

Librarians have been deeply involved in defining and refining their instructional role for the past decade and have developed a considerable body of knowledge on the subject. National organizations are dedicated to the dissemination of bibliographic instructional methodology and techniques through publications, symposia, and conferences.

Adams and Morris (1985) published their text before the full impact of assessment had been felt. Nevertheless, their description of the effective library user mentions goals and objectives closely related to the skills and competencies described by Ewell (1987b) and Boyer (Breivik, 1987). According to Adams and Morris, the effective library user can do the following things:

- Select and define researchable topics by considering background information, subtopics, alternative perspectives, and ways to determine whether there is enough information
- Set up efficient search strategies by selecting researchable topics, creating search terms, determining the most suitable tools, finding and using the tools, and locating materials
- Select materials appropriate for needed information and use footnotes and bibliographies to find more information.

Ewell's (1987b) cognitive and knowledge-building skills are thus clearly described as the outcomes of well-designed library instruction in Adams and Morris (1985).

Critical-Thinking Skills and Library Instruction

Lanning (1988), discussing the growing prevalence of legislation that mandates assessment of educational outcomes, proposes an answer to the question of how to quantify an increase in educational skills. Lanning suggests a generic response, one that can fit into the differing formats that outcomes assessment is assuming. He recommends that library skills be an important component of any educational assessment system. He points out (p. 8) that information skills "provide elements for critical thinking and . . . [help to] integrate diverse educational backgrounds," and he notes that level of skill is easily determined by pre- and posttesting.

As early as 1958, the concept of the library as a problem-solving instrument was being discussed: "The library is potentially one of the best integrative tools available. . . . The student . . . must bring a problem to solve, and he must use the resources . . . to find relevant materials, to evaluate the material, and to relate materials to each other to produce an organized answer. If the library is to fill this role, the student's approach to library usage must involve direction and the development and growth of skills. The library staff and the instructional staff must collaborate to develop this point of view in students" (Churchill and Rothman, 1958, p. 128).

Some of the groundwork leading to convergence of the goals of the teaching library and student assessment can be attributed to Library-College Associates, Inc., a nonprofit organization chartered under the laws of North Dakota in 1967, when a group of scholar-librarians—including the venerable Louis Shores, the avant-garde Robert Jordan, and the indefatigable Howard Clayton—proposed a number of unique and innovative concepts for the reform of liberal education. One of their design models posited the individualization of instruction in a library-centered, world-oriented ideal liberal arts college, where the library would serve as the laboratory of learning, and in which the roles of faculty and librarians would merge. Over the years, the visionary zeal of the library-college innovators has been shaped into a workable model that preserves the autonomy of faculty and librarians. The library-faculty partnership role has proved to be a realistic and effective approach.

Critical-Thinking Skills and Library Research Skills

One factor that has limited the development of library research as a formal academic discipline has been the lack of an operational definition of *critical-thinking skills*, to enable application of the theoretical construct. The potential has long been recognized. For example, Shou (1962, p. 69), writing on the teaching function of the university, refers to the role of the library as important because it is "not only the place to train students for acquiring logical and accurate thinking processes, but also the place for them to ask questions and to search for the answers."

Critical thinking and the role of the library are becoming increasingly interdependent. Knowles (1980, p. 28) suggests that "educators must rethink their roles and concentrate on teaching students the skills and attitudes needed for self-directed inquiry." The audience for Meyers's (1986) book is the instructional faculty, but the implied presence of a library-faculty relationship underlies many of the ideas and assignments proposed. For example, Meyers says (p. 1), "the amount of information available through computers and the media seems to have outstripped people's abilities to process and use that information. In such a context, colleges and universities need no longer serve as repositories of information, and teachers are no longer essential as lecturers and information givers. It is also increasingly important that students master the thinking and reasoning skills they will need to process and use the wealth of information that is readily at hand." Further, Meyers's definitions and descriptions of critical-thinking skills provide reinforcement for the techniques and processes currently valued in bibliographic instruction. For example, Meyers perceives the development of critical-thinking skills as analogous to the development of motor skills, which need regular practice and exercise, and he describes the process for designing instruction for that purpose:

> A central consideration in the design of any critical-thinking assignment is the building-block nature of critical-thinking processes. . . . Students do not learn to think critically merely by acquiring increasingly complex layers of discipline content, as traditional pedagogy assumes. Rather, they need to practice actively the component skills of critical thinking. They should begin with simple operations, such as summarizing, recognizing basic issues, identifying key concepts, and learning to ask appropriate questions. They can then build toward more complex and sophisticated skills, such as recognizing assumptions and creating and critiquing arguments. Learning to think critically is like developing any other skill. It must be practiced over and over again, at increasingly complex levels, before it is mastered [Meyers, 1986, p. 72].

Meyers's analysis holds important implications for the library-faculty partnership in the development of critical-thinking skills. The relationship between critical thinking and bibliographic instruction (BI) has been probed by Bodi (1988), who suggests that BI provides an appropriate structure in which to address critical thinking and that librarians can reinforce the ability to think critically "by making available a diversity of viewpoints . . . [and] by instructing students on how to find and evaluate these differing views" (p. 151).

Current Status of Libraries in Student Assessment

The potential, and the strengths, of effective library instruction for the curriculum and for assessment are increasing. In the spring of 1988, the Community and Junior College Libraries Section of the Association of College and Research Libraries surveyed its members on current professional issues. The survey included a section designed to elicit information about the role of the library in student assessment, as well as about connections between the library and the teaching of critical-thinking skills.

Of 360 respondents, 40 indicated that librarians at the colleges were deeply involved in the assessment process, and 35 reported that their institutions used—or planned to use—formal tests measuring competency in basic library skills. All twelve of the California community college libraries that returned survey forms reported libraries' involvement in the development of ways to assess critical-thinking skills. The following comments were selected from what respondents said about their involvement with and use of formal tests measuring competence in basic library skills.

California. "All of the librarians have met with faculty members who are key personnel in our collegewide effort on critical thinking, to discuss existing and needed resources and concepts of the effort and to open lines of communication for future evaluations." "Library instruction classes were revised to include the teaching of critical-thinking skills." "All course outlines are being rewritten to incorporate critical thinking. This year, a librarian has been chair of the college curriculum committee (on which a librarian always sits)." "All first-quarter students are required to take a library skills test, followed by library orientation."

Kentucky. "We plan to use a library skills pretest for English 101 students."

Michigan. "A library professional is codirector of a grant to bring assessment into the total curriculum." "We have a collegewide success-skills project to define, integrate, and evaluate outcomes in literacy, library skills, microcomputer skills, and critical-thinking skills."

New Jersey. "Both orientation courses include a library exercise section, which measures basic skills."

New York. "A library-faculty liaison works with the director of the Critical Thinking Program to select appropriate library materials. Tailor-made bibliographies and finding sources are constantly supplied for the program by the library faculty." "The library director wrote a grant to bring experts on critical thinking to the campus, to raise awareness of the issues."

South Carolina. "Library skills pre- and posttests are administered by each instructor."

Tennessee. "We are planning to do an entry-level assessment to measure knowledge of library skills." "A course in basic library skills is required of all students."

Vermont. "We have initiated a study of critical thinking and provided reading and study materials. We have also participated in a task-force piloting project. In addition, we teach a library course that emphasizes critical thinking."

Virginia. "Orientation contains a section on library skills, with a post-test." "We developed a self-paced library research course with a critical-thinking skills component and offered it collegewide in our multicampus institution."

Conclusion

The focus on assessment of educational outcomes will have an impact on curricular structure and coherence. Although many formats are being used to analyze and measure instructional improvement and accountability, most include emphasis on critical thinking, problem solving, and writing.

The educational or traditional "reference" function of libraries has become restructured and amplified, to emphasize the teaching role of the library. The discipline of bibliographic instruction has developed clearly defined goals and objectives, designed to contribute to the primary goal of the academic library: to support the curriculum of the institution. Bodi (1988, p. 151) advances a strong argument for BI in the college curriculum as "an appropriate teaching strategy to encourage and reinforce the development of critical thinking."

Breivik's (1987) efforts to foster library-faculty relationships through the development of course-related instruction have produced learning gains, positive attitudes, and the respectful attention of leading educators. McCormick (1983) has worked toward raising the standards of library instruction, proposing that the teaching of search strategies include evaluation of information.

The strength of the relationship between the library and the classroom has been shown, and the involvement of college librarians in student assessment should prove to be a valuable component of the process. Assessment can be used effectively in developing the full potential of the college library. In turn, the unique contributions of well-developed bibliographic instruction can enhance the assessment process. The opportunity is at hand for gains to the institution and to the library, through dialogue and through partnerships between faculty members and librarians working together to achieve mutual and institutional goals.

References

Adams, M., and Morris, J. *Teaching Library Skills for Academic Credit*. Phoenix, Ariz.: Oryx Press, 1985.

Bodi, S. "Critical Thinking and Bibliographic Instruction: The Relationship." *Journal of Academic Librarianship*, 1988, *14* (3), 150–153.

Breivik, P. S. "Making the Most of Libraries." *Change*, 1987, *19* (4), 45–52.

Churchill, R., and Rothman, P. "Extraclass Experiences." In National Society for the Study of Education, N. B. Henry (ed.), *The Integration of Educational Experiences. Fifty-Seventh Yearbook of the Society*. Vol. 47, Part 3. Chicago: University of Chicago Press, 1958.

Ewell, P. T. "Assessment: Where Are We?" *Change*, 1987a, *19* (1) 23–28.

Ewell, P. T. "Establishing a Campus-Based Assessment Program." In D. F. Halpern (ed.), *Student Outcomes Assessment: What Institutions Stand to Gain*. New Directions for Higher Education, no. 59. San Francisco: Jossey-Bass, 1987b.

Finn, C. E. "Trying Higher Education: An Eight-Count Indictment." *Change*, 1984, *16* (4), 29–33.

Knowles, M. *The Modern Practice of Adult Education: From Pedagogy to Andragogy.* (Rev. ed.) Chicago: Follett, 1980.

Lanning, J. A. "The Library-Faculty Partnership in Curriculum Development." *College & Research Libraries News*, 1988, *49* (1), 7–10.

McCormick, M. "Critical Thinking and Library Instruction." *RQ*, 1983, *22*, 339.

Meyers, C. *Teaching Students to Think Critically: A Guide for Faculty in All Disciplines.* San Francisco: Jossey-Bass, 1986.

Shou, S. T. "Teaching Function of a University Library." *Improving College and University Teaching*, 1962, *10* (2), 69–71.

Gloria Terwilliger is director of learning resources at the Alexandria campus of Northern Virginia Community College.

Library skills instruction is being integrated into writing classes in response to new developments in literacy and technology, which call for teaching both subjects as a process that emphasizes problem solving and critical thinking.

Vital Connections: Composition and Bibliographic Instruction Theory in the LRC

Lori Arp, Kathleen Kenny

The community college LRC contains perhaps the only library environment in which the staff must educate students to use libraries in *other* institutions. Preparatory students will go on to research library environments and casual students to their local public libraries, while graduates employed in large companies will utilize their special or corporate libraries. Therefore, the role of the LRC must include teaching information-retrieval concepts through some form of bibliographic instruction (BI) that approaches library research as a transferable process. Traditionally, bibliographic instruction programs in community colleges have been linked with the curriculum through English composition courses.

For librarians involved in instruction, it has become increasingly clear that familiarity with current BI theory alone is insufficient. To integrate bibliographic instruction successfully into composition courses, one must also keep abreast of developments in composition theory and be able to articulate parallels between the two fields to faculty and administrators. This chapter views trends in composition instruction and parallel developments in the field of BI and recommends an approach to incorporating these concepts into future program design.

Evolving Concept of Literacy

The development of students' literacy skills is a primary goal of community colleges. Although most people tend to associate the concept of literacy with the most common dictionary definition of a literate person—"an educated person, one who can read and write"—that definition has been constantly evolving and under scrutiny by experts. Hillerich (1982, p. 53) recalls that in 1976 literacy was defined as "that demonstrated competence in communication skills which enables the individual to function, appropriate to his age, independently in society with a potential for movement in that society."

Nevertheless, as Clifford (1984, p. 479) notes, scholars have recently come to view literacy more broadly, as a continuum where "at one end lies some ability to reproduce letter combinations with voice or hand, at the other end, such language-using behaviors as are called logical thinking, higher-order cognitive skills, and reasoning." Clifford also points out that historians now seem to agree that the development of literacy is "highly context-specific and context-dependent." Computer literacy, for instance, has evolved as one such context-specific type. In any case, the definition of literacy continues to evolve as society's need to access information increases.

Ability to Access Information: A New Form of Literacy

Because of the information explosion, the importance of the ability to gather information—to access, retrieve, and evaluate it—now constitutes a significant part of the definition of literacy. In the near future, individuals who are unable to locate information will be equally illiterate as those who are now unable to read or write. Their actions and opinions will be uninformed and frequently ill defined. Even now, college-educated people can no longer rely on previous knowledge, textbooks, and faculty to provide all the information they need for informed opinions; no individual or group is capable of assimilating all that is available. Instead, the ability to gather information independently and appropriately will determine socioeconomic mobility and, ultimately, the upper range of the continuum of literacy itself.

The information literacy movement has been, in part, an attempt to articulate the role of libraries and librarians in promoting literacy. In March of 1987, the first National Symposium on Libraries and the Search for Academic Excellence addressed this topic. Participants included higher education faculty and administrators, librarians and library educators, and representatives of business, government, and educational associations. Breivik (1987, p. 46), reporting on the symposium, emphasizes one consensus item: "Better undergraduate education means better integration of libraries in the learning process."

Teaching Composition and Critical-Thinking Skills

Composition instructors have responded to these new definitions of literacy by demonstrating primary concern with the relationship between the development of writing skills and critical-thinking abilities. Young (1978) reports that instructors are now teaching the process of writing (classical rhetorical invention), rather than evaluating the products of writing. Larson (1982) notes that they are designing assignments that can be based on students' expertise and addressed to a real audience, rather than creating arbitrary academic exercises. Flower and Hayes (1981), for example, describe writing as a set of cognitive processes, while Bruffee (1986) emphasizes the social dimension of writing, stressing that teachers who require written assignments are initiating students into various language communities, with parallel language conventions and assumptions about voice and lines of reasoning.

Writing-Across-the-Curriculum Programs and Microcomputers

The writing-across-the-curriculum movement, which involves composition instructors in helping their colleagues develop students' writing skills in subject-related assignments, has integrated these various trends, emphasizing both the importance of writing as a tool for learning and the need to teach students how to transfer language abilities from one knowledge domain to another. Instructors are now also using networked microcomputers to transform the college classroom from a teacher-centered, passive environment into a student-centered, collaborative workshop. The growing use of word processing in the composition curriculum is an important example of the use of new technology for freeing faculty to concentrate on the content, rather than on the mechanics, of students' writing. In 1984, 51 percent of entering freshmen had written a computer program within the previous year. Their increasing familiarity with computers will force instructors to continue investigating potential instructional applications of new technology.

Bibliographic Instruction for Critical-Thinking Skills

Teaching critical-thinking skills—especially on the basis of educational theory—has long been of concern to BI librarians. Aluri and Reichel (1984), for instance, discuss behaviorism and cognitive theory and their impact, past and potential, on bibliographic instruction. Kobelski and Reichel (1981) describe seven types of conceptual, cognitive frameworks for BI, involving type of reference tools; systematic literature searching, general or specific; form of publication; primary and secondary sources; publication sequence; citation patterns; and index structure.

Just as composition instructors have moved toward writing as a process, librarians now see research as a recursive or "re-searching" process. Mellon (1984), developing a generic model of library research, uses Flower's three-stage model of cognitive writing processes and examines parallels for each stage. The model has been used in freshman composition classes at the University of Tennessee, and it would be appropriate for many other types of composition classes as well. It presents the library as one solution to the problem of insufficient knowledge. While students learn to summarize, paraphrase, and prepare bibliographies, they are also learning the cyclic process of searching out, retrieving, and evaluating information.

The Association of College and Research Libraries/Bibliographic Instruction Section (ACRL/BIS) (1987) uses a conceptual approach that emphasizes the process of information gathering. Another useful search strategy, developed at the University of Illinois and described by Arp and Wilson (1984), incorporates a hierarchical system of goals and subgoals into its cognitive approach to information retrieval.

Renewed emphasis on providing information-access skills at time of need, rather than on creating arbitrary academic exercises or "treasure hunts," is exemplified in the work of many librarians (Mellon, 1984; Henry and Leather, 1986; Wilson and Arp, 1984) who use a modular, course-integrated approach to instruction. Community college librarians at Glendale, Arizona (Williams and Miller, 1986), and Miami–Dade, Florida (Watters, 1986), have described programs that address the parallels between reading and writing and bibliographic instruction across the curriculum.

In four-year colleges and universities, efforts have focused on providing instruction in the context of the student's major discipline. Keresteszi (1982) outlines a model of the development of disciplines and describes the corresponding literature produced at each stage. Reichel and Ramey (1987) describe ways in which BI can be integrated into subject disciplines in the humanities, social sciences, and sciences. Although community college librarians have not yet adopted this approach, the widespread involvement of the two-year colleges in writing-across-the-curriculum programs will probably require librarians to focus more attention on discipline-based research in the future.

Integrated BI for Critical-Thinking Skills at Auraria

At the Auraria Library, we have begun to integrate critical-thinking skills into the curriculum through a sequence of courses offered by the Community College of Denver's English department. The librarian introduces increasingly sophisticated critical-thinking and research skills into a series of program offerings for English 108, 109, 121, and 122. In English 108, the librarians provide students with a general overview of the library and its services. In English 109, they incorporate critical-thinking skills through the preresearch skills instruction (PRSI) program. PRSI students are asked to research and write a "minipaper," with materials and topics chosen for them in advance. During instructional sessions, students become aware of the qualities of different materials used in literary research, and they are required in their papers to synthesize the divergent views presented. The writing instructor works with the students continuously during the reading and writing process, helping them identify and summarize key ideas presented in the literature and incorporate their individual views and beliefs on the topic.

In English 121, librarians introduce students to the concept of the discipline and to the different materials that make up the literature of the various disciplines. Librarians and instructors select one multidisciplinary topic for students to analyze, as well as one general magazine article and four articles from journals of different disciplines. Students must examine the different viewpoints, writing styles, and research methodologies of all the disciplines represented. They are also asked to make personal decisions about the relevance of different methodologies and points of view. Class discussions frequently involve such questions as these: What is science? How does it differ from social science or technology? Students then write essays summarizing what they have learned from the articles, the librarian's lecture, and the discussion.

In English 122, the librarians link a series of writing assignments to research assignments. The research assignments are based on the ACRL/ BIS model statement of objectives for academic bibliographic instruction and use a research strategy developed at the University of Illinois (Arp and Wilson, 1984). Four class sessions are held in the library as the students begin their writing and research projects.

The first session typically occurs when students are asked to document an expository essay. The librarian discusses the use of expert opinion to document an argument, portraying the academic library as repository of expert testimony organized according to discipline. Students are encouraged to use subject encyclopedias as appropriate sources to find out what the experts in different disciplines believe to be the essential information about topics. The librarian describes the general characteristics of a subject encyclopedia. It consists of signed articles, which often include the author's credentials; provides overviews of topics for the layperson, from a disciplinary point of view; defines the jargon of the field; and often includes bibliographic citations to the core literature. The librarian then helps each student locate, analyze, and summarize articles from two subject encyclopedias relevant to the topic.

In another library session, students begin to investigate magazine and newspaper articles related to their topics. The librarian defines the role of popular periodicals as to entertain and inform, pointing out that the impaired credibility of these publications ultimately limits their usefulness as information sources for academic assignments. Students learn the process of finding periodical articles in the Auraria Library and spend at least half of the class period working with the newspaper indexes and the

Readers' Guide to Periodical Literature. As in all sessions, access terminology and concepts are stressed. For example, the librarian explains that indexes, computer data bases, and library catalogues are designed to provide subject access, using either a thesaurus of controlled vocabulary terms or key words from the article title, abstract, or text. Students find that when they use controlled-vocabulary indexes they must pay attention to cross-references and changes in standard terminology. When they use key-word indexes they must be aware of synonyms, alternate word order, and word endings.

The following session introduces professional, technical, and scholarly journals. Their purpose—in contrast to that of popular periodicals—is to contribute to the permanent record of progress in the discipline and to serve as the main medium of communication informing and uniting investigators in the field. Since each discipline often has a corresponding index, the student must decide which discipline will probably be concerned with some aspect of the chosen topic.

Journal indexes typically strive for comprehensive coverage of the discipline, without regard to language or to the intellectual or technical level of the source publications. Nevertheless, librarians encourage students to adapt the skills that they have used in the other sessions to the search for journal articles.

The final session, sometimes scheduled a week or more after the preceding one, occurs when students are to become immersed in compiling bibliographies for a full-length research paper. This session focuses on a three-part research strategy, which encourages the student to repeatedly analyze the topic and the research process by discipline, depth of information needed, and type of source material required. Librarians discuss books and other retrospective materials and provide students with a thorough introduction to the on-line catalogue system.

Together, these programs build skills progressively. Students learn to evaluate materials critically and to understand the concept of discipline as it applies to the literature. They learn that different experts have different styles and definitions of truth. Students are encouraged to begin to articulate their own views of the world in the context of scholarly research. We have found not only that the concept of the academic discipline can and should be taught at the introductory level but also that community college students understand and are intrigued by the complex world of the literature of the various disciplines.

Impact of New Technologies on Composition and BI

While composition instructors have been investigating the impact of new technologies (such as microcomputers and word processing) on the process of writing, instructional librarians have been examining the impact of on-line catalogues, on-line bibliographic data bases (such as those of DIALOG or BRS), and CD-ROM data bases on the process of literature searching. Baker and Nielsen (1983), for example, describe the impact of using on-line catalogues on the retrieval process. Penhale and Taylor (1986) have reported on experiments with methods of integrating end-user searching (teaching students to search on-line data bases) into BI classes. King and Baker (1987) have identified important teaching concepts that can be transferred from print to electronic format, and they have called for more studies to examine correlations between the ways students use new and traditional technologies and methods. Finally, Reese (1988) has reported on a comparative study of the differences in how students use print products and their CD-ROM counterparts.

Impact of Program Assessment on Composition and BI

In community colleges, the recent emphasis on program assessment has had a significant impact on the development and design of composition courses. Resnick and Goulden (1987, p. 5), outlining the history of program assessment, find it "linked to the ebb and flow of public confidence in the nation's schools and colleges." This issue came to national attention in 1983, when the National Commission on Excellence in Education called for a serious "back to basics" approach. Program assessment has the potential to affect the teaching of composition either positively or negatively. The national attention that assessment has focused on the need for developing students' writing skills has found support in interest from major funding sources, but if program assessment is not carefully implemented, it may result in curricula that are designed with no faculty participation except at the administrative level.

The problem of measuring the success of BI programs has been examined extensively in the professional literature. The Association of College and Research Libraries/Bibliographic Instruction Section (1983) offers one of the best discussions of such assessment methods. The lack of long-range, longitudinal studies evaluating BI instruction, particularly with respect to students' retention of concepts and skills, continues to be a problem. Nevertheless, Kohl and Wilson (1986) have demonstrated the short-term success of BI, which uses a cognitive rather than a tool-specific approach.

Summary

Librarians have begun to implement many of the new developments in BI in community colleges. Although simply orienting students to a specific institutional library is considered an insufficient approach to BI, Coleman (1986) outlines ways in which conceptual approaches can be incorporated into the orientation program. Cammack, DeCosin, and Roberts (1979) discuss course-related BI in the community college. A variety of course-integrated approaches seem to be used frequently in community colleges (Southwick, 1985; Williams and Miller, 1986; Henry and Leather, 1986), but little appears in the literature about discrete, formal library courses in community colleges, perhaps because of the amount of time and preparation they require. These discussions are promising, but we still need more analysis of the success or failure of programs and their structure in the professional literature.

Examination of recent trends in composition and bibliographic instruction demonstrates that important theoretical progress has been made in both areas. Specifically, both fields are concerned with broadening definitions of literacy to encompass critical-thinking skills, problem-solving skills, and access to information. Scholars in both fields are experimenting with the teaching of critical-thinking skills through a process approach that acknowledges the differences in how disciplines view research and writing. The use of new technologies in research and writing is being evaluated. Finally, the national move toward program assessment in higher education is affecting both fields.

The parallels in thought and experimentation between these two fields are obvious. In most cases, however, professionals in each field are working in isolation, establishing a body of literature that reports primarily to others in that field. Future cooperation depends on increased communication between the library and the writing departments. Since librarians must thoroughly understand the goals of composition programs as well as those of libraries, the burden of initiating cooperation is likely to fall to librarians. The learning resources center, through its mission of teaching and its strong traditional ties to learning centers and writing programs, is in a unique position to take a leadership role in communication and experimentation with these new directions.

References

Aluri, R., and Reichel, M. "Learning Theories and Bibliographic Instruction." In C. A. Kirkendall (ed.), *Bibliographic Instruction and the Learning Process: Theory, Style, and Motivation.* Ann Arbor, Mich.: Pierian Press, 1984.

Arp, L., and Wilson, L. "Librarian's Viewpoint—Theoretical." *Research Strategies,* 1984, 2, 16–22.

Association of College and Research Libraries/Bibliographic Instruction Section. *Evaluating Bibliographic Instruction: A Handbook.* Chicago: American Library Association, 1983.

Association of College and Research Libraries/Bibliographic Instruction Section Task Force. "Model Statement of Objectives for Academic Bibliographic Instruction: Draft Revision." *College & Research Libraries News,* 1987, 48 (5), 256–261.

Baker, B., and Nielsen, B. "Educating the Online Catalog User: Experiences and Plans at Northwestern University Library." *Research Strategies,* 1983, 1 (4), 155–166.

Breivik, P. S. "Making the Most of Libraries." *Change*, 1987, *19* (4), 44–52.

Cammack, F. M., DeCosin, M., and Roberts, N. *Community College Library Instruction.* Hamden, Conn.: Linnet Books, 1979.

Clifford, G. J. "Buch and Lesen: Historical Perspective on Literacy and Schooling." *Review of Educational Research*, 1984, *54* (4), 472–500.

Coleman, P. "Give 'em the Big Picture: Bibliographic Instruction for Freshman Orientation." *Research Strategies*, 1986, *4* (3), 132–135.

Flower, L., and Hayes, J. L. "A Cognitive Process Theory of Writing." *College Composition and Communication*, 1981, *32* (4), 365–387.

Henry, M., and Leather, V. "Bibliographic Instruction Across the Curriculum." *Community & Junior College Libraries*, 1986, *4* (3), 45–53.

Hillerich, R. "Towards an Assessable Definition of Literacy." *English Journal*, 1982, *65* (2), 50–55.

Keresteszi, M. "The Science of Bibliography: Theoretical Implications for Bibliographic Instruction." In C. Oberman and K. Strauch (eds.), *Theories of Bibliographic Education: Design for Teaching.* New York: Bowker, 1982.

King, D., and Baker, B. "Human Aspects of Library Technology: Implications for Academic Library User Education." In C. A. Mellon (ed.), *Bibliographic Instruction: The Second Generation.* Littleton, Colo.: Libraries Unlimited, 1987.

Kobelski, P., and Reichel, M. "Conceptual Framework for Bibliographic Instruction." *Journal of Academic Librarianship*, 1981, *7* (2), 74–77.

Kohl, D. F., and Wilson, L. A. "Effectiveness of Course-Integrated Bibliographic Instruction in Improving Coursework." *RQ*, 1986, *26*, 206–211.

Larson, R. L. "The 'Research Paper' in the Writing Course: A Non-Form of Writing." *College English*, 1982, *44* (8), 811–816.

Mellon, C. "Process Versus Product in Course-Integrated Instruction: A Generic Model of Library Research." *College & Research Libraries*, 1984, *45* (6), 471–478.

National Commission on Excellence in Education. *A Nation at Risk: The Imperative for Educational Reform.* Washington, D.C.: U.S. Government Printing Office, 1983.

Penhale, S., and Taylor, N. "Integrating End-User Searching into a Bibliographic Instruction Program." *RQ*, 1986, *26* (2), 212–220.

Reese, C. "Manual Indexes Versus Computer-Aided Indexes: Comparing the *Readers' Guide to Periodical Literature* to *Info Trac II.*" *RQ*, 1988, *27* (3), 384–389.

Reichel, M., and Ramey, M. A. (eds.). *Conceptual Frameworks for Bibliographic Education.* Littleton, Colo.: Libraries Unlimited, 1987.

Resnick, D. P., and Goulden, M. "Expansion, Quality, and Testing in American Education." In D. Bray and M. Belcher (eds.), *Issues in Student Assessment.* New Directions for Community Colleges, no. 59. San Francisco: Jossey-Bass, 1987.

Southwick, N. S. "Development of a Curriculum-Integrated Library-Use Instructional Model: A Systematic Approach." Unpublished dissertation, Nova University, Fort Lauderdale, Fla., 1985.

Watters, R. D. "A Climate for Excellence: Paving the Way for Student Success at Miami–Dade South's Library." *Community & Junior College Libraries*, 1986, *4* (4), 7–27.

Williams, J. J., and Miller, L. A. "Glendale Community College Instructional Materials Center: A Model for Student Success." *Community & Junior College Libraries*, 1986, *4* (4), 29–33.

Wilson, L., and Arp, L. "Librarian's Viewpoint—Practical." *Research Strategies*, 1984, *2*, 23–32.

Young, R. E. "Paradigms and Problems: Needed Research in Rhetorical Invention." In C. R. Cooper and L. Odell (eds.), *Research on Composing: Points of Departure.* Urbana, Ill.: National Council of Teachers of English, 1978.

Lori Arp is coordinator of instructional services for Auraria Library, which serves one two-year and two four-year academic institutions in Denver, Colorado. She served as chair of the ACRL/BIS Task Force on the Model Statement of Objectives for Academic Bibliographic Instruction in 1987.

Kathleen Kenny is science librarian at Auraria Library.

State-mandated assessment, testing, and literacy efforts will require LRC staff to work with developmental faculty in creating integrated assignments for increasing numbers of underprepared community college students.

Role of the LRC in Developmental and Literacy Education

Margaret Holleman, Julie Beth Todaro-Cagle, Barbara Murray

Involvement of community college LRCs in the developmental education and literacy efforts of their institutions has been inadequate over the years (Rippey and Truett, 1983-84; Phifer and Person, 1983; Gerhardt, 1985-86) and is now attracting professional concern because of mushrooming enrollments of nontraditional students and national and state efforts regarding adult literacy and admissions and placement testing (Todaro-Cagle, Martinez, Dubin, and Murray, 1989).

In 1982, the Secretary of Education estimated that, in addition to large numbers of immigrants and refugees for whom English is not the primary language, there were 72 million American adults functioning at or below marginal levels of literacy (Phifer and Person, 1983). More recent reports indicate that 20 percent of the population is illiterate. Moreover, a large proportion of the students who pass tests at minimal levels in basic reading and science lack the critical-thinking skills to analyze the material they read and learn. In this information age, employers are alarmed by gross misspellings on the résumés they receive and by the inadequate vocabularies and poor communication skills of those they interview.

As a result, at least twenty-one states have established testing at some level (admissions, placement, "rising junior," exit, "no pass, no play," "value added") to achieve educational reform. State and national governments are funding various programs to combat illiteracy. During the past three years,

---

This chapter is partly based on a presentation by the authors and Eileen Dubin at the American Library Association convention in Dallas, June 1989. Eileen Dubin's remarks have been incorporated into Chapter Eleven.

NEW DIRECTIONS FOR COMMUNITY COLLEGES, no. 71, Fall 1990 © Jossey-Bass Inc., Publishers

23

the ABC and PBS television networks have been sponsoring prime-time dramas and one-minute spot announcements to highlight the problem of illiteracy and recruit volunteers for various associations to help fight it.

Nontraditional students—minorities; those with job or family responsibilities; disabled people; academically, economically, or culturally disadvantaged persons; reentry women; adult workers who need to upgrade their job skills or launch second careers; non–native speakers; prisoners—have found expanded opportunities in open-door colleges (Cohen and Brawer, 1982). Many, however, will be identified by assessment tests as requiring specific kinds of basic remedial instruction, as well as counseling, advising, and tutoring, before they can begin participating in regular academic or vocational programs and courses.

Types of Remedial Programs

Literacy Education. The literacy movement encompasses native speakers who read below the sixth-grade level and non–native speakers who either have limited English abilities or cannot understand, read, speak, or write English. The latter group requires basic competency in understanding and speaking English before being able to begin working toward functional literacy. Most schools use a "language experience" approach and consider a student's writing literacy level equivalent to his or her reading level.

Work-Force Literacy. Corporations that hire those who are illiterate or non–native speakers may offer on-site literacy instruction tailored to employees' jobs.

Adult Basic Education and Adult Secondary Education. ABE is for those who have not graduated from high school and who read at the eighth-grade level or below. Adult secondary education is for adults who also lack a high school diploma but who read at the ninth- through twelfth-grade level.

Remedial/Compensatory/Developmental Education. Students who have completed high school and take community college entrance tests that show their reading level to be at tenth- to twelfth-grade proficiency or below, or who lack basic skills in writing and mathematics, require *remedial* classes to be able to enter regular college programs. *Compensatory* programs address deficiencies or disadvantages in students' sociocultural environments. *Developmental* programs are intended "to meet students where they are and take them to where they want to be by teaching both academic and human skills" (Phifer and Person, 1983, p. 11).

LRC Involvement in Developmental Education

Literature on this topic indicates that while most community colleges have well-established developmental education programs, with many constituting separate academic divisions, the libraries and LRCs have only minimal involvement with the programs. LRCs tend to make passively available such related service as multimedia collections; alternative course-delivery systems; electronic carrels for self-paced study; space for tutoring and classes; high-interest/low-vocabulary, ethnic, and citizenship materials; and computer-assisted instruction.

Some LRCs operate or contain learning, enrichment, tutorial, or survival-skills centers or labs. Studies indicate that integrated library instruction improves academic achievement and retention rates of developmental students (Rippey and Truett, 1983-84). Nevertheless, one survey of California community college LRCs found only 1 percent of library instruction aimed at developmental students. Another study, of Texas community college LRCs, reported that, on the average, librarians were involved with developmental students only 2.5 hours per week (Rippey and Truett, 1983-84). Librarians tend to point to inadequate funds and staffing, as well as to their own lack of expertise, to explain such findings.

Professional Calls for More Active LRC Involvement

Various professional groups have recently called for more direct involvement of LRCs and librarians in developmental and literacy programs. For instance, the librarians who prepared *Alliance for Excellence* (1984) recommend that public and community college libraries cooperate in state and local coalitions against illiteracy, teaching adults "how to compute, cope, and survive" in a learning society (p. 31), while simultaneously conducting research "on the best teaching strategies for literacy training" (p. 34). They also advise that college and university libraries be staffed with strong advisers who can both "lead students toward advanced learning skills" and "offer remedial help in basic information skills" (p. 29).

The Committee on Services to the Disadvantaged of the Community and Junior College Libraries Section (CJCLS) of ACRL published a draft statement (1987, p. 189) on the role of the library/LRC in educating basic-skills students. It uses the following definition of basic-skills students: "Students [who] are severely limited in life choices because they lack the basic skills essential for lifelong learning. In an earlier era they might not have graduated from high school and almost certainly would not have gone on to college." The committee recommends direct involvement of librarians with developmental faculty in identifying basic-skills students and designing individualized library assignments to reinforce the basic skills that students are learning. CJCLS has also created a new committee to address literacy across the curriculum.

The proposed new "Standards for Two-Year-College Learning Resources Programs" (1989) imply the inclusion of involvement with developmental education in the LRC's mission statement. They also specify the provision of instruction and services to all levels of users. Further, they call for "building and maintaining collections that adequately support . . . needed remedial programs" (p. 503) for nontraditional or underprepared learners.

Successful LRC Developmental Education Programs

A number of successful LRC-initiated programs have been reported in the literature. One at the Kingsborough Community College (New York) LRC contains many of the elements deemed necessary for success: librarians, faculty, and tutors collaboratively designing and implementing remedial instruction that incorporates visual aids, handouts, hands-on practice, and research on real-life issues (Schneider and Fuhr, 1982).

Suarez (1985) describes an information skills lab created at Miami-Dade's North Campus LRC in 1983 for students in basic reading and writing courses. Librarians were responding to recent developments, which at their campus included high failure rates (50 percent to 70 percent) on state-mandated entry and exit testing, college-mandated standards for student academic progress, and significant ethnic-minority enrollment (over 72 percent). The college president, moreover, had redesigned the educational program to emphasize the skills necessary for success and competence in the information age. Suarez conceives of the ideal remedial program as administered in the LRC by librarians, who help faculty design self-paced lessons that emphasize guided reading and writing activities in general studies.

Librarians at Chattanooga State Technical Community College (Tennessee) became successfully involved in providing integrated instruction in remedial classes because some of the minimum competencies students had to achieve were in specific library skills, such as locating items in the catalogue and the *Readers' Guide*, using features of books and reference works, and gathering information from primary and secondary sources (Houck, 1988). Librarians there build sequentially on this basic set of library skills as students progress through the remedial classes and into regular English classes (Henry and Leather, 1986).

Model Library/Developmental Education Program

Although a variety of successful models exist, one that is realistically attainable by most community college LRCs with current levels of staffing, training, and funding has been developed at Austin Community College's (ACC) Rio Grande Campus. Other successful models include nonlibrary enrichment centers, tutorial programs in the library, special collections, and a variety of arrangements for cooperation with various programs. ACC's program concentrates on faculty librarians and developmental teaching faculty combining forces for cooperative classroom curriculum development and teacher training.

ACC's proactive arrangement involves faculty librarians sitting on developmental curriculum task forces and revision committees. Librarians also serve as members of developmental faculty interview committees and as speakers and trainers in workshops designed to educate full- and part-time developmental faculty.

With the goal of at least one library exercise in each developmental class, faculty work together to isolate reading and writing skills not covered well or at all in developmental reading and writing texts. (Specific reading skills they have identified include identifying content that represents purpose and tone, detecting bias and propaganda, and evaluating arguments.) Once they have isolated specific skills that have not been covered, faculty identify and assess the reading levels of relevant materials in the library's general and reference collections and design exercises for the classes.

A key element of this process is the teaching faculty member's involvement in preparing students, handing out assignments, and including assignments as an integral part of courses. After this preparatory process, students visit the library individually to complete exercises, which require them (according to the level of the class) to use the library catalogue and some indexes but always involve them in interacting with librarians.

ACC's model is realistic for its own LRC and would be for most others because it does not involve expanded space needs, specialized educational backgrounds for librarians, ongoing funds for special collections, visits to developmental classes each semester (which would require high staffing levels), or massive curriculum revision for developmental faculty. This realistic approach integrates library skills into the curriculum as well as into instruction already in place in nondevelopmental classes. The program directors advise librarians not to "reinvent the wheel," but rather to build on successful examples of library instruction from other locations and on curricular areas of developmental education. They feel that if librarians are flexible and initially accept any degree of cooperation or interest from developmental faculty, close cooperation will ensue as developmental faculty recognize the types of contributions that librarians can make.

Readers' Advisers. Developmental faculty teach students basic skills, and librarians can help by recommending library materials that students can use to practice those skills and to develop the type of "cultural literacy" (Hirsch, 1987) and background they will need when they move into regular college programs. Developmental teachers generally deplore the quality of their texts and prefer to offer their students more compelling, exciting reading material.

Assessing Library Skills and Readability Levels. Since library or information literacy is not yet included in the various types of formal assessment testing, librarians need to be able indirectly to assess remedial students for such skills—ideally, through library assignments. To design such tests and recommend appropriate reading materials, librarians need to learn how to assess readability levels, not only of books and tests but also of directions and menus used in library software programs, on-line public catalogues, and CD-ROMs. User-friendly, inexpensive microcomputer programs are available for measuring readability levels.

Collection Development. Once librarians are able to assess readability levels, they should attempt to develop their collections of high-interest/ low-reading-level materials in all subject areas. At the College of DuPage (COD), a program with eight public libraries (which, with COD, comprise a literacy education consortium) experimented with new-reader collections. It was found that these materials received much greater use if they were integrated into the general library collection but were clearly identified on the shelf and in bibliographies with some kind of standard logo.

Appropriate Environment. A comfortable, caring environment is extremely important for developmental students, most of whom are reluctant to seek help, have poor self-concepts and past histories of failure, and feel powerless. Wyman (1988) suggests the use of staff specifically trained in and identified with library developmental services.

Integrated Instruction. All studies indicate that the most effective library instruction is integrated into regular class assignments, after a model developed at Earlham College (Farber, 1974) and highlighted at periodic conferences for teams of librarians, instructors, and administrators.

Special Instructional Techniques. The instructional techniques most effective with remedial students include teaching in teams, using various audiovisual materials, reinforcing sequential instructions with handouts, distributing outlines with blank spaces for note taking, remembering students' names and research topics and providing them one-to-one assistance and frequent positive reinforcement, and seating them at round tables for group work. Librarians can obtain sample lessons from the LOEX Clearinghouse at Eastern Michigan University. A full-text data base of materials on developmental education, called LINDEX, may also soon be available.

Successful Literacy Programs

In Illinois, the Secretary of State directed that literacy education be carried out through existing libraries and school systems. Therefore, community colleges and public schools have cooperative agreements with public libraries to provide literacy programs, with state funding for literacy and volunteer services. Community colleges also receive grant funds for disadvantaged students from the state community college board.

The adult basic education program at the College of DuPage is part of a nine-member district library literacy coalition that provides literacy education for native speakers who read below sixth-grade level and for non-native speakers with limited English speaking, writing, and reading abilities. The goal for the latter group is to help them achieve sixth-grade competency. These students can enroll in credit classes or simply work with volunteer tutors.

Volunteer tutors and classroom aides are crucial to literacy education. Volunteers normally must complete training programs and agree to work a minimum number of hours each quarter or semester. The College of DuPage has 330 volunteers for literacy to work with 1,200 students. The core group of tutors consists of retirees, but a growing number are young professionals, many of whom take a personal interest in the students and serve as excellent role models. COD, for instance, has been able to team up a Spanish-speaking North American engineer with an engineer from Ecuador, and a Chicago doctor of Polish extraction with a husband-wife doctor team from Poland who want to pass the examinations necessary to practice medicine in the United States. COD also has intergenerational programs, in which volunteers provide tutoring and child care to adult students so that they can read books aloud to their preschool children.

Brehm (1984) describes another long-established and successful volunteer tutoring program at Portland Community College, which employs almost 600 volunteers as tutors or classroom aides. The program is directed by two certified volunteer supervisors, one for ESL and one for ABE.

Conclusion

A few LRCs have taken the lead in providing special instructional services for developmental and literacy students. Perhaps because of mandated admissions testing and exit testing in Florida, learning centers in that state tend to be coming back gradually under the umbrella of community college LRCs, and this may prove to be a trend. In any case, librarians can no longer ignore the needs of the burgeoning numbers of nontraditional and underprepared students, who by the year 2000 will make up at least 40 percent of community college enrollments. More faculty librarians need to learn not only how to teach but also how to form instructional teams to create integrated assignments. Perhaps the graduate library schools and professional associations will modify their curricula and workshop offerings to help future public and academic librarians acquire such skills.

The challenge for LRCs is clear. Students enroll in developmental and literacy programs, not to get new or better jobs, but to feel better about themselves and to be able to make more of their own life choices. These are the kinds of students who can benefit most from the types of information accessing and critical-thinking skills LRC staffs must begin to offer, in partnership with instructional faculty.

References

Alliance for Excellence: Librarians Respond to A Nation at Risk. Washington, D.C.: U. S. Department of Education, 1984. 71 pp. (ED 243 885)

Brehm, D. "The Volunteer Tutoring Program at Portland Community College." *Community & Junior College Libraries,* 1984, 3 (1), 25–33.

Cohen, A. M., and Brawer, F. B. *The American Community College.* San Francisco: Jossey-Bass, 1982.

Committee on Services to the Disadvantaged of the Community and Junior College Libraries Section of the Association of College and Research Libraries. "Library Services to the Academically Disadvantaged in the Public Community College: A Draft." *College & Research Libraries News,* 1987, *48* (4), 189–191.

Farber, E. I. "Library Instruction Throughout the Curriculum: Earlham College Program." In John Lubans, Jr. (ed.), *Educating the Library User.* New York: Bowker, 1974.

Gerhardt, S. L. "Library-Administered Remediation: One Program That Works." *Community & Junior College Libraries,* 1985-86, *4* (2), 41–44.

Henry, M., and Leather, V. "Bibliographic Instruction Across the Curriculum." *Community & Junior College Libraries,* 1986, *4* (3), 45–48.

Hirsch, E. D., Jr. *Cultural Literacy: What Every American Needs to Know.* Boston: Houghton Mifflin, 1987.

Houck, T. "Library Skills Instruction for Developmental Courses." *Community & Junior College Libraries,* 1988, *5* (2), 53–56.

Phifer, K. O., and Person, R. J. "The Role of Community College Libraries and Learning Resource Centers in Literacy Education." *Community & Junior College Libraries,* 1983, *2* (1), 9–22.

Rippey, D. T., and Truett, C. "The Developmental Student and the Community College Library." *Community College Review,* 1983-84, *11* (3), 41–47.

Schneider, A., and Fuhr, M. L. "The Library's Role in Remediation: A Cooperative Program of Physical and Philosophical Integration at Kingsborough Community College." *Community & Junior College Libraries,* 1982, *1* (2), 47–58.

"Standards for Two-Year College Learning Resources Programs: A Draft." *College & Research Libraries News,* 1989, *50* (6), 496–505.

Suarez, C. C. "The Library and Remedial/Developmental/Compensatory Education: A Case Study." *Library Trends,* 1985, *33* (4), 487–499.

Todaro-Cagle, J. B., Martinez, D., Dubin, E., and Murray, B. "Responding to the Needs of Developmental Students." Panel presented at the American Library Association convention, Dallas, Texas, June 1989.

Wyman, A. "On My Mind: Working with Nontraditional Students in the Academic Library." *Journal of Academic Librarianship,* 1988, *14* (1), 32–33.

Margaret Holleman is director of library services at the West Campus of Pima Community College, Tucson, Arizona. She has been editor of the quarterly Community & Junior College Libraries *since its inception in 1982.*

Julie Beth Todaro-Cagle is head librarian at Pensacola Junior College's Learning Enrichment Center.

Sister Barbara Murray is director of Pensacola Junior College's Learning Enrichment Center.

Librarians are joining faculty in efforts to internationalize the curriculum, expand the concept of community, and generate a global perspective in students and the public.

The LRC's Role in Helping Faculty Internationalize the Community College Curriculum

Liz Bailey, Nancy E. Buchanan, Margaret Holleman

In today's world, the only certainties are change and the recognition that continuous learning and adaptation are essential for survival. Community colleges face many challenges in preparing students to function in a rapidly changing environment. One of the most exciting and demanding of these is providing an internationalized education.

The Need for International Education

The need for a citizenry with international knowledge and competencies has long been argued as crucial to this country's national security, economy, and image. Students need an international education in order to effectively function as citizens in a democracy. It is impossible to understand contemporary events or issues, let alone make intelligent choices or decisions, without a well-structured knowledge of the world.

Today, the United States has more immigrants crossing its borders than in any other period of its history. Therefore, students need an internationally based education to understand and appreciate the cultural mix found in their own communities. In recent years, moreover, foreign investments in the United States have skyrocketed, and multinational corporations have established themselves throughout the nation. Many communities are also increasingly recognizing the importance of foreign tourism to their local economies.

Foreign students now make up one-third to one-half of enrollments in

NEW DIRECTIONS FOR COMMUNITY COLLEGES, no. 71, Fall 1990 © Jossey-Bass Inc., Publishers

departments of some colleges and universities. In 1987–1988, there were 46,053 foreign students in two-year institutions, 80 percent of them in twelve states: California, Florida, Texas, New York, Virginia, Massachusetts, Illinois, Maryland, Washington, North Carolina, Arizona, and New Jersey. Miami-Dade enrolled 5,148, and Northern Virginia enrolled 1,650 (Ziko-poulos, 1987). At Bunker Hill Community College (Boston), almost 40 percent of the students are from Southeast Asia. In sum, cross-cultural understanding and communication skills are essential even to the American who never leaves the United States.

Links Between American International Business Competitiveness and Community College Education

As Americans have struggled to respond to new economic challenges, par-ticular attention has been focused on international education and American competitiveness in the world marketplace. To be competitive, Americans need an education that not only improves the technological performance of their businesses and industries but also provides them with knowledge about the global economy, international politics and law, cultural studies, and world geography, in addition to skills in foreign languages and cross-cultural communication.

The community, junior, and technical colleges are in a unique posi-tion to provide such knowledge and skills. First, they have a mission to provide vocational and technical training and retraining. Second, commu-nity colleges—because of their open-door philosophy, low tuition, and geographical proximity to students—are easily accessible and demonstrate a commitment, unreplicated anywhere else in the educational system, to lifelong learning. Over 1,200 community colleges in the United States enroll one-third of all students in higher education. Indeed, for a significant portion of the country's population, the community college is the only contact with higher education. Third, community colleges have a reputation for responding innovatively and quickly to the identified educational and training needs of local governments, businesses, and industries. Because community colleges train students for jobs, educate a significant portion of the population, and respond rapidly to training needs, they are in an excellent position to give American businesses a competitive edge by pro-viding an internationalized education.

Partnership in Successful International Programs

In 1976, the American Association of Community and Junior Colleges (AACJC) established the International/Intercultural Consortium, an ad-vocacy group that helps members enhance their programs by sharing information and resources. The group publishes a monthly newsletter, International Update. At the 1978 AACJC annual conference, the U.S. Com-missioner of Education called on community colleges to make a commitment to international education. Since that time, numerous two-year institutions have established or augmented international programs and consortia under grants from national and state governments and public and private foundations and agencies.

Establishing an international education program is, in many ways, a political process, which must be carried out in conjunction with local needs, interests, resources, and expertise. International education programs vary from institution to institution. Approaches may include study or travel abroad, work or study abroad, student and faculty exchanges, faculty and staff development, cultural concert exchanges, "sister" colleges or cities, hosted foreign training or technical assistance programs, international student clubs, foreign student or faculty mentoring and advising, community outreach, foreign-language and ESL programs, ethnic or international studies, and internationalized curricula.

Even the phrase *internationalizing the curriculum* does not mean the same thing at all institutions. Some institutions focus on developing separate and distinct new international courses and programs—in global, area, or ethnic studies or in international business and trade, for instance; others concentrate on infusing an international dimension into existing courses across all disciplines and programs. Whatever the approach, institutions with successful programs have recognized the following factors:

1. Faculty must be motivated to internationalize the curriculum and be internationally competent in their respective disciplines. For most institutions, this means developing and supporting a relevant faculty development program.

2. Faculty development must lead to curriculum development that systematically incorporates international material into the programs and courses so that it can reach students.

3. Good teaching faculty are the backbone of the programs, but they tend to be overextended, with heavy teaching and advising loads and active participation in professional organizations. To internationalize the curriculum, administrators must provide these faculty with committed support systems.

Recent studies (Boyd, 1986; Bronson, 1987; Diaz, 1985; Flax, 1982; Greene, 1982; Krasno, 1985; Robinson, 1985; Vassiliou, 1985; Wood, 1986) have described successful internationalization programs in community colleges. Although many provide instruction in international trade, the majority incorporate courses in foreign arts and culture into their foreign-language programs, or they infuse such materials in their study-abroad programs or in such classes as anthropology, geography, history, humanities, political science, sociology, or writing (Vassiliou, 1985).

Role of the LRC in Establishing Programs

LRC staffs have played a significant and vital role in international education efforts by providing research, expertise, and materials for grant writing, faculty development, curriculum and materials design, and other essential support services. As part of their philosophy or mission statements, community college LRCs invariably mention such ideals as supporting the philosophy and goals of the college (these often include encouraging students to take pride in their heritage and develop an awareness and appreciation of cross-cultural differences), providing faculty with support for their instructional programs, providing accessible collections of materials to meet users' needs, and providing a qualified, concerned staff to instruct people in the use of informational tools. Each LRC has developed its own system of fulfilling this mission as best it can, given the reality of its staffing and budgetary limitations.

Librarians committed to the concept of global literacy have taken the initiative in finding out what at their colleges is being done about international education. The LRC or library in most community colleges has a representative on the curriculum committee, who is in an ideal position to acquire relevant materials, be identified as a resource person in publicity for international programs, and make essential outreach efforts in the campus and community.

Wallace (n.d.) has outlined four general approaches to designing an international studies curriculum. The cultural approach stresses the social values reflected in art, history, language, and so on. The economic approach emphasizes world economic interdependence. The futurist approach focuses on global issues, and the political approach identifies patterns in international relationships.

Role of the LRC in Supporting International Studies

Faculty designing international courses who are using any of these four approaches can get support from the LRC in three ways: by participating in the selection of materials for international studies, by having the LRC provide easy access to such materials, and by working with librarians on specific activities to improve students' chances of completing assignments. Successful resource librarians have ascertained the specific research interests of involved faculty and learned what they expect of their students by asking for copies of their course outlines.

Many internationalized courses have taken an "adopt a country" or *cultural* approach, requiring students to use government documents, gather statistical and descriptive information, learn about the culture's life-style and values, and interview local diplomatic representatives. Drama and literature classes that incorporate the cultural approach require students to compare ways in which novelists or dramatists with different national styles have treated similar themes. Still other classes have students investigate the child-rearing customs and health practices of other countries.

Students in classes that emphasize the *economic* approach have had to develop skills in listening, nonverbal communication, and conflict negotiation, as well as in locating examples of foreign business reports and information on imports and exports. They have had to understand the basic concepts of international finance and law and to request information from foreign embassies or apply for jobs in foreign firms. Some have consulted issues of graphic-design publications and other reference works, in order to create advertising and newspaper layouts suitable for both the United States and other countries.

Classes designed around either the *futurist* or the *political* approach usually have students conduct research on such global issues as military disarmament, environmental pollution, energy production and consumption, and overpopulation. Whatever the approach, most of these classes have required significant research, as well as critical-thinking and problem-solving skills.

Faculty in the Southwest Consortium for International Studies and Foreign Languages (1985–1988) have utilized a library exercise in which students must define international terms and locate extensive information from a variety of sources about a selected country. Most faculty involved in international studies have found access to relevant information their greatest need. Their success has depended on librarians' keeping them abreast of materials to support their course outlines. Many organizations, publications, and programs provide valuable resources for international studies and global education; a comprehensive outline of them is available in Hoopes and Hoopes (1984). Librarians have also familiarized faculty with community resources and asked to be put on the mailing lists of such organizations as Global Perspectives in Education, Inc., the Institute of International Education, the Institute of Latin American Studies at the University of Texas, and the Center for Japanese Studies at the University of California (Berkeley).

An LRC can easily create an international studies center in a filing cabinet, giving students and faculty easy access to sample international-studies course outlines from other colleges; bibliographies of available multimedia materials, classified by subject and country or region; lists of available grants, study-abroad, or student-faculty exchange opportunities; information about career opportunities for bilingual persons; lists of publishers and audiovisual producers specializing in foreign materials; free travel brochures available through *Travel/Holiday* magazine and foreign embassies; lists of research centers specializing in intercultural education; files of resource speakers; and calendars of local appearances by such foreign entertainment groups as the Teatro de Danza Española or the Shanghai Acrobats. Librarians can also provide faculty access to on-line data bases that are international in scope, such as *Social SciSearch, Foreign Trade & Economic Abstracts, World Affairs Report, PAIS,* and *PTS International Forecasts.*

Since acquiring new materials for international programs puts an added strain on most LRC budgets (modest to begin with), librarians have often acquired foreign-language materials through international students. They can also acquire free publications, such as *Korea Today, Canada Today, Pakistan Affairs,* and *Ghana News,* from foreign embassies or promote such relatively inexpensive periodicals as *Business America, Americas, China Pictorial, In Britain,* or *Africa Report.* Popular European magazines, such as *Paris Match* and *Epoca,* always seem to be popular in libraries. Such materials are helpful to librarians who have worked closely with faculty teaching classes in foreign languages, cultural geography, the history of Eastern civilizations, and the history of Mexico, classes that traditionally have been in college curricula but are also a vital part of international studies.

Activities of LRC Staff in International Education

A number of community colleges have programs similar to one at Lansing Community College (LCC) for Chinese faculty fellows. Begun in 1986, in collaboration with the World Bank, this program has brought about twenty faculty and administrators each year from technical colleges in the People's Republic of China to LCC, where they have been paired with faculty mentors. They come to investigate the design and teaching of LCC's voc-tech courses in order to establish or upgrade programs in their own two-year institutions.

The director of the learning resources center at LCC served as mentor to a Chinese librarian who, like the other faculty fellows, audited classes recommended by her mentor, attended ESL classes, and participated in a class in curriculum designed and taught by a Chinese professor from Michigan State University. The mentor also had this librarian study the functional areas of the LRC, learn basic on-line searching techniques, and conduct a survey of the attitudes of part-time faculty about the LRC and its services. The LRC director and her staff designed a library orientation class for the faculty fellows and another for their international students, both of which are still being used.

At Valencia Community College, a similar program—FLORICA—promotes the exchange of faculty, education, culture, and commerce between Florida and Costa Rica. In its art gallery, Valencia's LRC recently featured works by Rudy Espinoza, engraving master of the Universidad Nacional in Heredia, who provided workshops and lectures for students and the general public at three local community colleges.

A reference librarian at Kirkwood Community College (Iowa) was recently selected by international program staff to coordinate the dissemination of information on international education opportunities, and the resource librarian at Pima Community College has participated in several regional, noncredit seminars and workshops and worked closely with faculty advisers of organizations for international students. Finding that the instructors of Pima Community College's classes for travel agents were alarmed by recent surveys indicating widespread illiteracy among students with respect to global issues and world geography, the resource librarian arranged to have the students read fiction and nonfiction about their countries and regions of interest. Another Pima librarian, in Argentina on a grant, has been invited to participate in that country's planning for community colleges.

At Brevard Community College (Florida), the dean of LRCs designed and hosted one of his college's summer study-abroad programs specifically for local librarians. They toured six European nations and visited museums, libraries, and consulates. Similarly, the resource librarian at Shoreline Community College (which, like many other Washington State two-year institutions, has been involved in business training programs with Pacific Rim countries) prepared herself for involvement in international studies by spending a year's sabbatical traveling around the world and attending conventions of the International Federation of Library Associations and Institutions.

In 1987-1988, a faculty committee at the South campus of Miami-Dade Community College began creating its Cultural Enrichment Archives Collection. Committee members are raising funds to purchase materials— for now art books and exhibition catalogues, but eventually examples of ethnic arts and crafts—that will reflect the countries of origin of their international students, primarily Latin and South America and the Bahamas. Initiated and chaired by a faculty member who is also an art critic and a writer for *Art International*, the committee includes three librarians and the LRC director. Like many LRC staffs in schools with significant international programs and populations, those at the Miami-Dade campuses set up elaborate exhibits and activities during the heritage weeks held for various ethnic groups throughout the academic year.

Conclusion

The shrinking world community, as well as surveys indicating widespread ignorance among students and the general populace about global issues and world geography, have affirmed the need for colleges to forge a link between what students are learning in the classroom and what they are learning in the world at large. International education is an essential component of the community college mission. Internationalizing the curriculum means a significant commitment of time, energy, and resources. Community college instructional and LRC faculty can form a mutually beneficial partnership, helping their institutions respond to this challenge and extend the concepts of community and classroom.

References

Boyd, C. M. *Institutional Opportunities Plan for International Development.* Jacksonville: Florida Community College, 1986. 76 pp. (ED 276 482)

Bronson, O. *Internationalizing the Curriculum: Curriculum Handbook.* (Rev. ed.) Tucson, Ariz.: Southwest Consortium for International Studies and Foreign Languages, 1987.

Diaz, C. "Improving International Relations: Is There a Role for Community Colleges?" *Community and Junior College Journal,* 1985, 55 (4), 32–37.

Flax, S. "Integrating the Humanities and Business Education: The Experience of International Business as an Example." Paper presented at the annual convention of the American Association of Community and Junior Colleges, St. Louis, Mo., Apr. 1982. 15 pp. (ED 216 732).

Greene, W. *Report on the International Education Program at Broward Community College.* Fort Lauderdale, Fla.: Broward Community College, 1982. 8 pp. (ED 216 731)

Hoopes, D. S., and Hoopes, K. R. (eds.). *Guide to International Education.* New York: Facts on File, 1984.

Krasno, R. "The Contributions of the Community Colleges to International Education." Speech delivered to the Annual Conference on International Education, Lake Buena Vista, Fla., Feb. 1985. 23 pp. (ED 256 379)

Robinson, B. S. "New Dimensions in Intercultural Education at Community Colleges." Paper presented at "Focus on the World: Meeting the Educational Challenge of the Future," Bridgewater, Mass., 1985. 9 pp. (ED 273 338)

Southwest Consortium for International Studies and Foreign Languages. *Incorporating International Knowledge and Competencies into the Undergraduate Curriculum.* Tucson, Ariz.: Southwest Consortium for International Studies and Foreign Languages, 1985–1988.

Vassiliou, E. "Parameters of International Studies." *Community and Junior College Journal,* 1985, 55 (4), 14–17.

Wallace, S. A. *Infusing International Components Curriculum Workbook.* Tucson, Ariz.: Pima Community College International Awareness Project, n.d.

Wood, S. V. *International Business Education Programs in the California Community Colleges: Final Report of the Project. 1985/86.* Berkeley, Calif.: Peralta Community College System, 1986. 140 pp. (ED 274 384)

Zikopoulos, M. (ed.). *Open Doors 1987/88: Report on International Educational Exchange.* New York: Institute of International Education, 1987. 189 pp. (ED 303 117)

Liz Bailey is director of international education at Pima Community College, Tucson, Arizona.

Nancy E. Buchanan is the resource librarian for the international program at Pima Community College.

Margaret Holleman is director of library services at Pima Community College.

*The 1990s offer LRCs exciting opportunities to expand their
historical involvement in institutional faculty and staff development
programs, which strongly influence the quality of instructional and
support programs.*

LRC-Based Professional Development

Howard Major

Jackson Community College (Michigan) is typical of higher education institutions today. Like others, it faces the following challenges, requiring the
provision of effective, user-centered professional development and renewal
for faculty members, administrators, and staff:

- National demographic changes, including the aging of the higher education work force, and reduced mobility and increased burnout among
overextended community college professionals (American Association of
Community and Junior Colleges, 1988; Cohen, 1986; White, 1981)
- Extensive use of part-time employees, especially part-time faculty, who
currently comprise 60 percent of the community college teaching corps,
and who need to be integrated into the institution (American Association
of Community and Junior Colleges, 1988; Hoenninger and Black, 1978)
- The major role that faculty and staff play in maintaining and renewing
institutional and community vitality (Williams, 1977; American Association of Community and Junior Colleges, 1988)
- Maturation of a research-based body of knowledge about effective teaching, and selection and use of instructional strategies
- Public demand for institutional quality and accountability, requiring program assessment and faculty evaluation
- Rapidly emerging and evolving electronic information and communication technologies (Needham, 1986)
- Public pressure for the type of higher education that will transform and
rejuvenate the American economy

NEW DIRECTIONS FOR COMMUNITY COLLEGES, no. 71, Fall 1990 ©Jossey-Bass Inc., Publishers

- Global interdependence, requiring an international perspective within higher education institutions
- Recommendations calling for curriculum consultants to play a role in articulation efforts with public schools
- Accelerating rates of change in almost every aspect of society, which affect all academic communities.

Indeed, the American Association of Community and Junior Colleges (1988) calls for innovative responses to many of these changes, noting that the average full-time community college faculty member is now fifty years old, has taught at least ten years, carries a heavy load of five courses per semester, and adapts constantly to accommodate instruction to the widening diversity among students and to keep abreast of dramatic developments in technology, world affairs, and subject matter.

Until recently, Jackson Community College has also been typical of higher education institutions in its traditional methods of addressing the professional development needs of faculty and staff members: by scheduling inservice presentations or workshops, sending employees to occasional off-campus conferences and meetings, and asking each new full-time employee to participate in a one-time orientation that clarified college procedures and policies. These traditional approaches have certain strengths, but they also have some important limitations. For instance, on-campus presentations are normally scheduled for specific times, and they address one or several preselected topics. This sort of inflexible scheduling and narrow focus make the participation of many employees, full- and part-time, inconvenient or unlikely. Many may not have a pressing need for the information or may not find the topics appealing; hence the typically low attendance at professional development presentations, and the correspondingly low percentage of employees served by such programs. Morever, like staff at many community college LRCs (Harnish, 1986; Platte and Dassance, 1981; Watts, 1981), the staff at Jackson Learning Resources Center have long supported such traditional activities by supplying full- and part-time faculty and staff with "professional reading collections," citations to relevant current articles and publications, and in-depth assistance with their continuing education and research projects, and by participating in the college's orientation programs. Here the similarity ends, however.

To overcome inflexible scheduling, narrow focus, and low utilization of the college's traditional professional development program, staff members of the Jackson Learning Resources Center have established the Professional Development Center. Designed, implemented, and maintained under the auspices of the LRC, it uses such instructional technologies as videotapes, audiotapes, and computers for presentations. It is designed to serve all categories and levels of college personnel and is continually available as a drop-in center where employees can select informational programs at times of greatest need and convenience.

Professional Development Materials

The drop-in center has materials available in such familiar and easy-to-use formats as videocassettes and audiocassettes, slide-tapes, filmstrips, video-discs, and microcomputer software, in addition to print. Employees have easy access to information which can be selected, organized, and displayed in menu mode. The hundreds of professional development topics include college policies and procedures, classroom instructional strategies, supervision and leadership skills, administrative and management techniques, program planning and budgeting, long-range planning, employee wellness, effective use of emerging technologies, and incorporation of innovative processes.

To access this information, any full- or part-time employee comes to the center at a convenient time, selects an area of interest from the menu of professional development topics, and receives a guide from an LRC-based instructional developer. This guide facilitates the employee's subsequent independent use of the center's collection of materials by providing an introduction to the chosen topic, suggestions for related objectives, objective-referenced learning activities and materials, an optional self-test or checklist, and a bibliography. All the information and materials are designed to be self-instructional, so that users can engage in independent learning, but the LRC also uses its instructional developers to personalize the professional development experience and provide employees with desired interaction and feedback.

Some of the materials are commercially produced; others are developed by college employees. The center conducts traditional formal and informal needs assessment to determine whether to acquire or produce the materials. When it is best to create materials, the center identifies college employees who have relevant expertise and offers them a small financial incentive to work on presentations with LRC-based instructional developers and technicians. The resulting sense of investment and pride in the LRC tends to increase employees' use of it.

Motivating Staff to Use the Center

A representative, collegewide advisory committee, consisting of full- and part-time teaching faculty, administrators, and support staff, actively guides the development of the center. The chair of the LRC has taken an active role in the center's development and implementation, incorporating it into the college's long- and short-range plans, goals, and objectives. The college has provided the necessary facilities, equipment, personnel, and funds to assist the center's implementation.

Existing and planned incentives to promote use of the center include certificates of accomplishment and financial rewards to be conferred when employees implement professional concepts that they have learned at the center. The center makes financial awards to college staff, not just because of their participation in its activities but also for any behavioral changes brought about by their participation.

Evaluation of the Center

Evaluations of the center will focus on the following anticipated outcomes for the college and its staff:

- Extended support for employee-developed professional growth plans
- Expanded ability to address individual staff members' professional needs and interests
- Enhanced empowerment of employees through their increased control over their own professional development
- Improved job-related performance
- Increased positive attitudes toward work
- Increased understanding of and adherence to college policies and procedures, with subsequent reduction in the institution's legal vulnerability
- Optimized use of the college's financial and human resources
- Improvement of instructional and support programs.

Evaluation of the center begins with systematic collection and analysis of feedback from users and eligible nonusers. In addition to addressing the intended outcomes just listed, the evaluation includes a goal-free component to identify any unanticipated outcomes. The long-range goal of evaluating the contexts, resources, processes, and products of the project is to assess the extent to which staff use what they learn in the center and, by extension, the extent to which the center's activities benefit students.

The drop-in center is an extremely cost-effective approach to the crucial task of providing comprehensive staff development. It uses staff's existing expertise in producing and presenting materials. By permitting staff to design their own professional development plans, choose the topics of greatest significance to them, and schedule their own participation, it makes efficient and effective use of staff time. It also makes optimal use of existing materials and facilities.

Other institutions could easily adopt this concept. Barshis (1984) notes that professional development programs like this one, programs that take place within a systematic organizational development effort, are the ones most likely to succeed. Virtually all higher education institutions have LRCs, or libraries staffed with personnel who are trained in the selection, organization, production, and dissemination of instructional materials.

Many LRC staff also have specific training in instructional and/or professional development.

In many cases, the drop-in professional development center could be established simply through reorganization of existing material and human resources. The drop-in center offers a participative approach to institutional staff development and provides LRCs exciting opportunities to address some crucial challenges of staff development in the wider context of increased institutional assessment and accountability.

References

American Association of Community and Junior Colleges. *Building Communities: A Vision for a New Century.* Washington, D.C.: American Association of Community and Junior Colleges, 1988. 58 pp. (ED 293 578)

Barshis, D. *Assisting Student Learning.* Los Angeles: Center for the Study of Community Colleges, 1984. 6 pp. (ED 251 139)

Cohen, A. M. *Perennial Issues in Community Colleges.* Paper presented as part of a seminar series at North Carolina State University, Raleigh, Apr. 1986. 18 pp. (ED 270 139)

Harnish, D. *Focus on Faculty: A Report on Professional Development at Niagara County Community College 1985–86.* Sanborn, N.Y.: Niagara County Community College, 1986. 23 pp. (ED 286 570)

Hoenninger, R., and Black, R. A. "Neglect of a Species." *Community and Junior College Journal,* 1978, 49 (3), 25–27.

Needham, R. L. *Are Communications Technologies in Education a Threat to Faculty?* Los Angeles: ERIC Clearinghouse for Junior Colleges, 1986. 6 pp. (ED 269 114)

Platte, J. P., and Dassance, M. A. "The PRC: A Professional Library for Professional Decisions." *Community College Frontiers,* 1981, 9 (3), 49–51.

Watts, G. E. *Faculty Resource Guide.* Fort Smith, Ark.: Westark Community College, 1981. 39 pp. (ED 205 250)

White, K. B. *Deferred Maintenance or Institutional Renewal? Professional Development Leaves at Valencia Community College.* Orlando, Fla.: Valencia Community College, 1981. 46 pp. (ED 205 251)

Williams, R. W. "Development of a Plan for the Implementation of a Faculty Development Program at Malcolm X College." Ed.D. practicum, Nova University, Fort Lauderdale, Fla., 1977. 45 pp. (ED 148 455)

Howard Major is department chair, Learning Resources Center, Jackson Community College, Jackson, Michigan.

LRCs must be creative in providing support for the increasing numbers of off-campus, distance-education classes made possible by new technology for nontraditional students.

LRC Support for Off-Campus Education

W. Lee Hisle

All types of academic institutions offer extension and distance-education programs, which permit students to earn college credit without attending classes on a campus. Community colleges, because of their long-standing mission to serve nontraditional students through innovative means, often lead the way in implementing and supporting such education.

Students enrolled in distance education (DE) generally do not have face-to-face meetings with their instructors. DE traditionally has included *print-based, independent-study courses,* which have been offered in higher education for over fifty years; *radio courses,* which have been available for over thirty years; and *televised courses,* which have been offered on public education networks since the 1950s.

Today, DE is delivered via myriad telecommunications methods, limited only by a college's imagination, technological capabilities, and finances. For instance, courses are being offered via telephone, using a bridge connecting many students at once to the instructor's site. ITFS, a low-cost, limited-broadcast television technology, lets colleges transmit televised instruction over a twenty- to fifty-mile radius to cable systems, extension sites, or individual homes. Point-to-point microwave links permit colleges to send televised instruction to distant cable systems, ITFS transmission towers, or extension sites at local schools, industries, or prisons. Satellite uplinks and downlinks enable colleges to reach students in areas hundreds or thousands of miles distant.

Types of Distance Education

Telecourses—prerecorded video programs integrated with print and other media—comprise the most popular form of distance education, 200 having

NEW DIRECTIONS FOR COMMUNITY COLLEGES, no. 71, Fall 1990 © Jossey-Bass Inc., Publishers

been offered in 1987, and will probably continue to be popular through the turn of the century. They can be delivered via PBS or local cable channels or played on VCRs in learning centers or in students' homes. A 1986 survey of the use of 183 telecourses in 172 institutions showed that 81 percent of the respondents were two-year colleges, 94 percent of the telecourses were offered to undergraduates, 91 percent were offered for the same three hours of credit as similar campus offerings, and 27 percent of users provided a major print, video, or software instructional component (Brey, 1988).

Live, multisite instruction links students at several distant sites to the instructor through video, using cable, ITFS, point-to-point microwave, or satellite technology. One-way video, two-way audio is the most common format for these classes, but successful two-way video and audio systems, which permit students and faculty at all sites to simultaneously see and communicate with one another, are in operation at Kirkwood Community College in Cedar Rapids, Iowa (Wacker, Dennis-Burns, and Bunting, 1985) and at Kirtland Community College in Roscommon, Michigan (Perry, 1988). Another, at Jackson Community College (Michigan), is one of the first in the nation to be linked by fiberoptics technology (H. Major, personal communication, 1989).

Video teleconferencing, in the one-way video, two-way audio mode using satellite technology, is frequently used for continuing education and staff development. For instance, in 1988 the Community College Association for Instruction and Technology and the Community and Junior College Libraries Section of the Association of College and Research Libraries produced a national teleconference on CD-ROM technology. It was specifically aimed at LRC staff in 563 small community colleges in rural or remote locations, who frequently lack sufficient resources to attend workshops or conventions. Nevertheless, the receiving sites also included many larger systems, a comparable number of four-year college libraries, and some public schools and industries.

Electronic courses permit students to complete lessons on home computers, using modems to access college networks. Instructors provide feedback over this electronic link. Future types of DE will certainly employ interactive videodisc and hypermedia to bring images, text, and sound into the homes of students who have family and job responsibilities and scheduling and commuting difficulties.

Ramifications of Extension and Distance Education

All these systems deliver alternative types of instruction particularly convenient for those requiring professional development opportunities or for growing numbers of nontraditional students (including disabled students, those with academic, economic, or cultural disadvantages, or those with

job and family responsibilities who have scheduling and commuting difficulties). A survey of eight thousand students enrolled in forty-two different
telecourses, for instance, indicated that 44 percent were over age twenty-
nine, 68 percent were women, 81 percent were employed, and most had
dependents at home and were simultaneously enrolled in campus classes
but were taking the telecourses at home because of scheduling problems
(Brey and Grigsby, 1984).

Nontraditional students tend to be holistic thinkers, requiring an overall
context in which to place the material they are learning. They also have a
strong need for social interchange and a sense of community (Stove, 1985).
Recognizing this, Kirkwood Community College orients the instructors of
live, telelinked programs to place emphasis on students' participation and
involvement, both individual and group (Wacker, Dennis-Burns, and Bunting, 1985). Moreover, telecourses and other types of independent-study
programs are designed to be self-directed and require mature, self-motivated
students and responsive on-site faculty coordination and staff support
(Purdy, 1986). At most colleges, local instructors provide wraparound segments for telecourses and support for other types of independent study.

The types of outreach library services that LRCs design should also
respond to such needs, providing a strong human dimension and letting
students choose from a wide range of materials, in order to develop the
types of analytical thinking necessary to independent, lifelong learning
(Kascus and Aguilar, 1988; Boyer, 1987).

LRC Support Services for Distance/Extension Education

While extension and DE departments are increasingly innovative and successful in providing instruction to students at widely scattered, remote
locations, their college LRCs struggle to provide their faculty and students
comparable levels of support services: books, indexes, periodical articles,
reference assistance, audiovisual programs, software, microcomputers, audiovisual equipment, and study space (Gregor, 1984). Most accrediting commissions now expect colleges to provide comparable support services to
students at off-campus locations or in DE. The Off-Campus Library Services
Conference meets annually to discuss the problems inherent in doing so
(Kascus and Aguilar, 1988). The proposed "Standards for Two-Year College
Learning Resources Programs" (1989, p. 501) call for having off-campus
instruction at multiuse centers "supported by branch services or contract
services with an accessible library."

Colleges cannot realistically duplicate off campus all of the LRC support services available on campus and should attempt to make DE students
and faculty aware of this, perhaps by publicizing in catalogues and class
schedules a description of the types of basic support services they can
expect to receive at off-campus sites. Some states have identified such

basic services as core and reserve reading collections, professional library staff, supplementary materials, and adequate facilities (Kascus and Aguilar, 1988). Extension services may include contracting with nonaffiliated libraries to provide resources or services; using an off-site library office to provide consultations and access to reference materials, on-line searching, and interlibrary loan; establishing branch libraries; and providing bibliographic orientation and instruction, assistance with nonprint media and equipment, and reciprocal borrowing.

Such programs are difficult to initiate at sites where faculty have become accustomed to teaching with minimal or no library support. LRC services to DE students, moreover, are labor-intensive and require resourceful professionals who can provide access to bibliographic tools, collections, and assistance; design systems for rapid delivery of materials; and convince faculty they should make assignments for extended-campus students equivalent to those they make on campus (Kascus and Aguilar, 1988).

Model for Providing LRC Services to DE Sites

Austin Community College (ACC) uses a program development model (PDM) for DE services (see Figure 1). It encompasses most of the types of strategies used to varying degrees by community college LRCs and can be used by any LRC staff planning to improve or offer DE outreach services. It is also intended to guide the development of such programs. The PDM includes the following interrelated components.

Leadership. Extension services require ongoing, visible administrative leadership and commitment. This may simply involve granting release time to those responsible for developing and coordinating the services, securing the resources necessary to implement them, and monitoring the ongoing status of the program.

Familiarizing LRC Staff with DE Programs. LRC staff, particularly those responsible for designing and delivering outreach services, need to become familiar with DE courses and the methods used for their delivery, ideally through working with the administrators and faculty of the DE department. The DE and extension program administrators can supply important statistics about where DE students are concentrated geographically, identify the primary methods they use to deliver classes and the ways students typically receive them, and help the LRC categorize extension courses according to types of anticipated LRC support.

LRC staff need to interview DE instructors to find out how they have used libraries in the past and whether their requirements for DE students are different from those for on-campus students. Instructors' assignments—term papers, surveys, book reports, or other projects—indicate LRC services that their students will need, and book lists provide the basis for core, reserve, and supplementary collections.

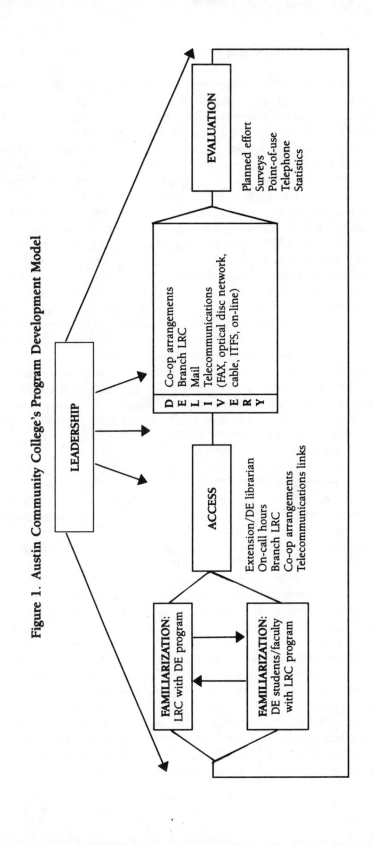

Figure 1. Austin Community College's Program Development Model

EVALUATION

Planned effort
Surveys
Point-of-use
Telephone
Statistics

LEADERSHIP

D E L I V E R Y

Co-op arrangements
Branch LRC
Mail
Telecommunications
(FAX, optical disc network,
cable, ITFS, on-line)

ACCESS

Extension/DE librarian
On-call hours
Branch LRC
Co-op arrangements
Telecommunications links

FAMILIARIZATION:
LRC with DE program

FAMILIARIZATION:
DE students/faculty
with LRC program

Familiarizing DE Faculty and Students with the LRC. A tenet of ACC's outreach program is that if you can lead a horse to water, he will drink . . . if he is really thirsty. If LRC staff can convince faculty and students of the value of knowing how to access information, orientation efforts will be more successful. LRC use, both on and off campus, tends to be faculty-driven. DE faculty can help market LRC services at orientation classes and can suggest items to purchase for the collection. LRC staff can mail promotional and informational materials about their services to DE students or incorporate that information into class syllabi, class schedules, or college mailings, including mailings of library materials. They can also insert short video clips explaining how to use the LRC at the beginning or end of a telecourse or a televised lesson. ACC has developed a short (four- to five-minute) video segment for off-campus students on using library research services. Such tapes can be edited for use in the classroom.

Access. Much of the DE program at ACC consists of telecourses or teleconferences. The college provides DE access to LRC services through the three main-campus libraries, through three branch-campus LRC centers, and through contracts with public and high school libraries.

All three main-campus LRCs provide telecourses or teleconference tapes, which students can view on VCRs. Contents of their combined general and reference collections are available at all campus and nonaffiliated libraries through the on-line public access catalogue (OPAC) module of the LRC's integrated, automated library system. Each of ACC's three branch campuses has a 1,000- to 2,500-square-foot LRC, with a basic support collection, reserve materials, telecourse tapes, study space, and part-time reference staff.

The LRC contracts with two large public library systems to house, in each of the main and branch units, two VCRs and tapes for thirty-five telecourses, in both VHS and Beta format. The LRC also pays the public libraries to provide ACC students with necessary equipment, storage space, free borrowing cards, and clerical assistance.

ACC places reserve collections and OPACs in four local high schools and contracts for faculty and students to use the high schools' audiovisual equipment, copiers, and telephones. Formal contracts with these nonaffiliated libraries, specifying costs for the types of services they provide, are the most successful.

Bibliographic instruction is provided in both on- and off-campus English composition classes, through a self-paced workbook that requires students to pick and narrow a topic for assigned research papers. Other possible access methods LRCs could provide are a toll-free number to the main campus, for obtaining reference assistance, photocopied or telefaxed articles, interlibrary loan, and renewal of circulated materials; micro-computer access to the LRC's OPAC, which would permit students to place holds on and request delivery of materials without staff assistance; and dial access from homes or extension sites to CD-ROM indexes. A number of community college libraries that subscribe to large microform magazine collections to support general indexes could easily mail or fax articles to other sites. Recent government-sponsored technology grants to community college LRCs support multitype library consortia activities, which should facilitate outreach efforts.

LRC staff should maintain statistics on the use of outreach services, to justify hiring full-time outreach librarians who can serve as direct liaisons between LRCs and extended-campus/DE faculty and students. All staff involved in outreach services need to be well informed about the college, its instructional programs, and its policies and procedures, in order to answer general questions. It is also valuable for LRC staff to stress that each branch or extension site is part of a larger service network.

Delivery. Contracting libraries and extension centers can serve as pickup points for materials sent from the main campuses by telefacsimile transmission, regularly scheduled college mail couriers, college vans, staff cars, public buses, or postal services. Colleges can also arrange with local cable franchises for addressable cable channels, so that nonsubscribers can receive (subject to copyright restrictions) college video or other audiovisual programming in their homes. Off-campus sites can obtain citations or even the full text of articles by having microcomputer access to on-line or CD-ROM data bases.

Fitzwater and Fradkin (1988) describe a consortium for sharing CD-ROM indexes and periodicals through Gammafax software and telefax machines. Greenberg (1987) describes a book-and-copy express van service employed by a group of academic and public libraries in New Jersey. Kirkwood operates a "tap line" to its main campus LRC, provides computerized listings of its library holdings and local periodicals to high school and public libraries near off-campus sites, mails requested materials, and publicizes services through videotapes, handouts, and posters.

The dean of learning resources at the College of DuPage envisions for the future an electronic mobile information center staffed by paraprofessionals and linked to the main campus by microwave. It would provide telephone access to librarians at the main campus and microcomputer access to the LRC's on-line public-access catalogue, career information programs, and various on-line and CD-ROM data bases. The main campus could fax articles to the center by microwave. Each morning, a van could stop at the local train station to permit service to commuters and then travel to one off-campus site, where it would stay for an extended time (Fradkin, personal communication, 1989).

Evaluation. Evaluation of off-campus LRC services is generally conducted haphazardly, if at all, as administrators go on to solve new problems once they have put complex programs into operation. Yet a systematic, ongoing evaluation, which reincorporates incoming data into a dynamic process of regeneration and revision, is essential to any program's success. Annual evaluation of LRC support for off-campus programs should incorporate data from a representative sample of faculty and students, indicating the degree of their satisfaction with access to materials and services. Such a survey should also familiarize users with available LRC services. It could be supplemented by in-depth telephone interviews with students and faculty, conducted by extension or DE departments. Colleges without staff and expertise could hire outside firms to collect and interpret such data.

Ongoing evaluation of the effectiveness and timeliness of services is possible through questioning of students and faculty as they pick up requested materials or as they enter and leave extension centers or cooperative library facilities. Staff can also use traditional methods of keeping statistics on numbers of intracampus and interlibrary loans and reference calls. The evaluation component of the model helps LRC staff to understand more about off-campus programs and to plan and improve services.

Conclusion

LRCs, in response to public expectations of excellence in education and various accreditation and professional standards for equitable services for nontraditional and off-campus students, must use innovative, creative methods of providing support for DE courses. Austin Community College's PDM offers a comprehensive systems model for planning, implementing, and evaluating such efforts.

References

Boyer, E. L. College: The Undergraduate Experience in America. New York: Harper & Row, 1987.

Brey, R. Telecourse Utilization Survey, First Annual Report: 1986–1987 Academic Year. Washington, D.C.: American Association of Community and Junior Colleges Instructional Telecommunications Consortium, 1988. 86 pp. (ED 301 295)

Brey, R., and Grigsby, C. Telecourse Student Survey, 1984. Washington, D.C.: American Association of Community and Junior Colleges Instructional Telecommunications Consortium, 1984. 61 pp. (ED 255 258)

Fitzwater, D., and Fradkin, B. "CD-ROM + Fax = Shared Reference Resource." American Libraries, 1988, 19 (5), 385.

Greenberg, E. "Book Express: Meaningful Access." College & Research Libraries News, 1987, 48 (9), 539–540.

Gregor, M.A.N. "The Provision of Learning Resources Services to Off-Campus Community College Students." Unpublished doctoral dissertation, University of Virginia, 1984.

Kascus, M., and Aguilar, W. "Providing Library Support to Off-Campus Programs." College & Research Libraries, 1988, 49 (1), 29–37.

Perry, S. B. "Interactive Instructional Technology Systems Development at Kirtland Community College, Roscommon, Michigan." Community & Junior College Libraries, 1988, 6 (1), 107–110.

Purdy, L. N. "Telecourses: Using Technology to Serve Distant Learners." In George H. Voegel (ed.), *Advances in Instructional Technology*. New Directions for Community Colleges, no. 55. San Francisco: Jossey-Bass, 1986.

"Standards for Two-Year College Learning Resources Programs: A Draft." *College & Research Libraries News*, 1989, 50 (6), 496–505.

Stove, H. "Reaching Adult Learners Through Public Television." Paper presented at the 36th annual meeting of the Conference on College Composition and Communication, Minneapolis, Minn., Mar. 1985. 8 pp. (ED 257 104)

Wacker, K. A., Dennis-Burns, J. D., and Bunting, D. R. "The Classroom . . . and the Library . . . That Cover Seven Counties." *Community & Junior College Libraries*, 1985, 3 (4), 23–32.

W. Lee Hisle is director of Learning Resources Services, Austin Community College, and current chair of the Community and Junior College Libraries Section of the Association of College and Research Libraries.

*Community college telecommunications centers have played a
dominant national role in producing high-quality telecourses in a
broad variety of subject fields to accommodate increasing numbers
of nontraditional students.*

Telecourses: Instructional Design for Nontraditional Students

Theodore W. Pohrte

Since the early 1970s, about 80 percent of the most widely used college
telecourses have been produced by five agencies: Coast Community College
District, Dallas County Community College District, the Maryland Center
for Public Television, Miami–Dade Community College District, and the
Southern California Consortium for Community College Television. Their
telecourses are used by more than one thousand two- and four-year colleges
and universities in the United States and Canada. They are also used in
United States overseas military installations and in English-speaking countries, such as Australia. Over the past sixteen years, enrollments in these
courses have exceeded one million.

The Annenberg/CPB Project, established by the Corporation for Public
Broadcasting (CPB) through a gift of $150 million from the Annenberg
School of Communications, has awarded grants since 1982 that have supported the production of outstanding telecourses and triggered the emer-
gence of new telecourse-production consortia. Annenberg-CPB productions
are carried by the Adult Learning Service (ALS) of the Public Broadcasting
System (PBS). PBS encourages its stations to persuade local educational
institutions to offer these telecourses to their students.

At present, however, the five principal producers—Coast, Dallas, Maryland, Miami–Dade, and Southern California—are providing a large portion
of the courses distributed by PBS/ALS. Four of these veteran producers also
market their telecourses to the Learning Channel, a satellite service that
delivers adult learning to cable TV companies and similar networks through-

---

The author wishes to acknowledge assistance from John A. Trickel.

out the United States and Canada and distributes directly to educational institutions, businesses and industries, the national government, and overseas users.

Telecourse Design and Production: Background

While producers may differ on the specifics, most follow the general kinds of procedures outlined in Levine (1987). This handbook describes a telecourse as an integrated instructional system, which normally consists of a television program with accompanying text, study guide, faculty manual, and examinations but which sometimes utilizes audiocassettes, computer software, a reader or anthology, or other print material.

Telecourse students enroll in an institution that has adopted the course and provides them with appropriate faculty and support services and academic credit. They work more independently than those in traditional classes, covering course materials at home or at work while receiving guidance from faculty by phone or mail or through special instructional techniques. Although telecourses require fewer class meetings, they are designed to be academically equivalent to traditionally taught college courses. Levine (1987, p. 10) highlights this necessary focus on academic quality: "Nationally available telecourses generally cost between one and several million dollars to develop, often involve world-renowned academic experts, instructional designers, researchers, and producers, and may take up to four years to complete. Decisions to begin course development, therefore, are not taken lightly. Further, since only course materials of the highest academic quality are likely to be adopted by colleges, academics are involved in significant ways throughout the development process."

Producing a Telecourse: Phase 1

Needs Assessment. Production of a telecourse at Dallas County Community College District (DCCCD) begins when the district and its Center for Telecommunications (CFT) conduct a needs analysis. District administrators first create an ad hoc faculty advisory committee of seven instructors in the subject area, one from each of its colleges in the district. If this committee endorses the proposal and CFT finds the potential for local enrollment and the strength of the national market encouraging, CFT submits a formal development proposal to the district.

Selection of Content Specialist. Telecourse producers often choose a principal content specialist from outside the college, frequently either the author of the text selected for the telecourse or another widely respected academic on the faculty of a four-year college or university. Nevertheless, DCCCD does interview internal candidates, looking for someone who not only has expertise in the subject field but who also demonstrates good interpersonal skills, willingness to take risks, and tolerance for frustration and ambiguity. One of these unique individuals is Dr. John Trickel, a historian who was chosen as content specialist for DCCCD's telecourse *The American Adventure.*

The content specialist first conducts a nationwide study on how the subject could be taught by telecourse, examining possible course goals, levels of instruction, principal content emphasis, and types of learning experiences. For instance, goals that Trickel identified for students to achieve in completing *The American Adventure* were (1) to gain a better perspective on the contradictions of the American experience, which has produced egalitarianism and slavery, opportunity and poverty, reform and reaction, immigration and nativism, and (2) to recognize one of the benefits of studying history, as a means of organizing and understanding the forces that influence people. At this point, DCCCD forms a local faculty advisory committee, made up of one subject specialist from each of its seven colleges (often those who have participated in the needs analysis), each of whom should demonstrate good team skills and enthusiasm for the project. The content specialist is expected to serve as the faculty coordinator and the advisory committee as the faculty for the telecourse when it is completed and first offered in the district.

Funding Telecourse Production. Funding patterns vary among producers. Coast, Miami–Dade, and Southern California use methods of funding similar to those of DCCCD, while Annenberg/CPB producers receive full, partial, or matching funding. Other producers depend largely or entirely on corporate or foundation underwriting.

At DCCCD, the CFT director enlists national partners—other institutions of higher education—in committing substantial resources to the project. Their contributions give them certain rights (perhaps for the lifetime of the telecourse) to use the materials. Some may receive a portion of the net income from the marketing of the telecourse, once development costs have been amortized.

The funding provided by each national partner also entitles one of its faculty members to participate in the telecourse's national faculty advisory committee, a group that provides the production with a national perspective. National partners with Dallas for *The American Adventure* were Amarillo College, Austin Community College, Coast Community College District, Florida State Department of Education, Higher Education Telecommunications Association of Oklahoma, Southern California Consortium, Tarrant County Junior College District, and Harper & Row Publishers, Inc. CFT also solicits contributions from public and private agencies, businesses, and industries. For this production, partial funding was provided by a grant from Frito-Lay, Inc.

Textbook Selection. One part of Dallas's funding pattern involves submitting requests for proposals to publishers of textbooks recommended by the content specialist. These requests describe ways in which the publishing house could participate in the project if its text were selected. In some cases, producers may select the textbook of the publisher offering the most attractive financial arrangement and design the telecourse around it. Others employ one or more academics to create a text or reader specifically for the telecourse. Occasionally a producer strikes an agreement with a publisher whereby the producer's content specialist can coauthor a new edition of the text or write an alternate version that better fits the goals of the telecourse. In the case of *The American Adventure*, the publisher of the text chosen by both the content specialist and the local and national advisory committees made the most attractive offer, providing a grant for producing the video elements, permitting the content specialist to be the principal manuscript reviewer for the text, enlisting the help of the text authors in developing the telecourse, printing and distributing the study guide (for which it paid the district a generous royalty), and participating in a comarketing campaign.

Production Team. At this point, CFT's manager of production services organizes a production team consisting of an experienced and nationally recognized producer of television documentaries, professional script writers, a professional videographer and editor, and assistants to the producer, as well as CFT's instructional design specialist, researcher, and directors of district telecourse operation and marketing.

At the close of the preliminary planning phase, the content specialist, the advisory committees, and the principal members of the production team develop a tentative blueprint for the telecourse, which outlines course level, content, goals, activities, and materials to support learning. Content is divided into twenty-six units, each of which will become a thirty-minute video element or telelesson. This is the common model for a one-term telecourse, although some employ several one-hour elements, while others comprise as many as forty-five half-hour video elements.

Producing a Telecourse: Phase 2

Script and Print Package Development. The content specialist gathers resource materials and generates outlines of the facts, concepts, and theories that will be presented in each lesson and that have emerged from tentative learning objectives established by the specialist and the faculty advisory committees. The instructional designer and the producer help the content specialist select one to three learning objectives to be emphasized in each telelesson. The remaining objectives are covered in the accompanying print materials. Scriptwriters use these outlines and materials to develop three- to four-page telelesson concept papers, which are reviewed and revised by most of the production team members, who continue to review subsequent first-draft scripts.

Selection of Host or Narrator. If the basic design of the series requires an on-camera and/or voice-over personality for studio or location shots, the production team screen-tests a number of candidates. These may include professional actors, faculty members, or the content specialist. The host must be able to instruct effectively on television. Many strongly prefer an academic authority in this role, but experience has demonstrated that an actor, who is better able to use the medium to communicate, is almost always more effective. Academics who are capable of performing well in this very demanding role, and who are also available and affordable, are rare. The actor Ryland Merkey was selected for *The American Adventure* because he was both comfortable and effective in the role of a mature, appealing, kindly storyteller, and he worked well with the series producer.

Evaluative Testing. Early in the process, some producers develop a prototypical lesson—a rough-cut, thirty-minute telelesson with corresponding study guide and text materials in approximately final form—which is then subjected to both formal and informal evaluation. Informal testing consists of having advisory faculty try out lessons with classes. Formal testing involves sampling, written questionnaires, and structured interviews. Levine (1987) lists the types of things that formative evaluations try to assess, including instructional level, academic rigor, wide academic and student appeal, appropriateness and effectiveness of course formats, corresponding levels of difficulty in both print and video portions, validity of content approach, compatibility with the existing curriculum, and effectiveness of production techniques (such as pacing and use of graphics, film footage, and experts).

Telecourse Production: Phase 3

While most DCCCD productions have combined location and studio shots, *The American Adventure* was shot entirely on location. The on-location production team consisted of the producer/director, the content specialist, the videographer, two audio technicians, and the narrator.

Two pivotal decisions had been reached early on: to have a series host trace United States history from its beginnings to 1877 at the original sites, and to incorporate the human dimension of primary sources (such as diaries, autobiographies, newspaper articles, minutes of meetings, memoirs, and so on). The latter were transcribed into first-person narratives, which were recorded onto the voice track by actors. The videotape was to consist of relevant art works, artifacts, and location shots and was to include interviews with nationally prominent historians who are considered authorities on this period of American history.

In one segment of the final product, viewers see a distinguished-looking gray-haired man standing before a Spanish cathedral and describing American soldiers celebrating a victory over Mexican troops in a busy square in the center of Mexico City. Viewers may take note of the appropriate scenery and the ambience it conveys, but few can appreciate the incredible logistics, hard work, resourcefulness, and serendipity that those few minutes of video represent.

This shot was the result of the first of ten filming trips, each of which lasted from four to fourteen days and required complex arrangements for connecting flights, car rentals, accommodations, permission to shoot, and interpreters.

For political, economic, and logistical reasons, the location team hired a Mexican production company to help shoot these segments and spent a great deal of time negotiating the terms of the contract. The fact that it had been raining for two weeks in Mexico City before the team arrived did not bode well for the project. On the first day, the team went to an excavation site in steady rain and rehearsed every time the rain slowed. Finally, when team members were about to begin shooting the scene, they learned that the Mexican producer had not had time to pick up the tapes that the team had sent from Dallas four weeks earlier.

The second day's expedition took the team out of the rain and into the National Archaeological and Anthropological Museum, to shoot a huge model of the ancient Aztec capital, Tenochtitlan. Because the museum previously had had trouble with thieves, security was tight, and the team had trouble getting in, not to mention setting up lights and equipment and redirecting museum traffic. After a few disagreements, the team managed to leave with the footage it wanted.

Filming from the Great Plaza before the cathedral had to be conducted in a beehive of activity, with vendors, visitors, schoolchildren, and vehicles all crowded together, and it was interrupted by a heavy downpour. Despite all the problems, the group left Mexico City with ten cassette tapes.

Each day was broken down and scheduled, just as each script was divided and assigned. Sometimes geography proved difficult, as when the team was filming the opening of the series at the magnificent ruins in Chaco Canyon, New Mexico. The team's accommodations were sixty miles away, and half that drive was over unpaved roads.

At another location, bad weather proved serendipitous. When rain and mosquitoes made it impossible for the crew to film the host at a rice field near Charleston, South Carolina, he was filmed walking along a sandy trail, and he recorded the voice track separately. Those hauntingly beautiful background shots were a powerful introduction to the topic of slavery in the colonial South.

Prominent American historians were interviewed in their homes (although Edmund Morgan of Yale had to be interviewed in a field outside his summer home in New Hampshire, because the cabin lacked adequate power). The fact that they could not use prepared notes during the interviews created some difficulties with timing and unanticipated responses.

All in all, the production team spent 107 days on the road, working at the mercy of bad weather, extreme heat and cold, equipment failures, communications problems, ambient noises, inadequate maps, and intrusive onlookers (Trickel, 1988).

Telecourse Production: Phase 4

In this final phase of production, staff complete the final editing and "audio sweetening" of the telelessons. They also give the print elements their final revisions, and the content specialist and the instructional designer prepare the test-item bank and the faculty manual. Faculty advisers continue their review and critique throughout this phase. During the production process, CFT markets the telecourse through promotional brochures, preview booklets, newsletters, conference exhibits, and advertisements. Because community college practices in telecourses for nontraditional learners are constantly evolving, readers may wish to keep abreast of work done by the principal producers in this field.

References

Levine, T. K. *Teaching Telecourses: Opportunities and Options, a Faculty Handbook.* Washington, D.C.: Annenberg/CPB and PBS/Adult Learning Service, 1987.

Trickel, J. A. "Making *The American Adventure.*" Unpublished notes, 1988.

Theodore W. Pohrte is director of instructional services, Center for Telecommunications, Dallas County Community College District.

A central instructional role for the learning resources center can result from the community college's dedication to achieving excellence in education through promotion of active learning and use of experiential labs in all disciplines.

Active Learning and the LRC

Richard L. Ducote, Alicia T. Tibbals, Steven E. Prouty

Reminiscent of the heady days when new community colleges were springing up, in the 1960s and 1970s, the opening of Collin County Community College (McKinney, Texas), in 1985, was marked by great optimism, vision, and a determination to address a nationally recognized need. From the time of the college's conception, its founders were determined to build a learner-centered institution of educational excellence where students would be actively involved in their own learning.

After three years, the college had two permanent campuses, with a student population exceeding five thousand, and was planning a third campus. Situated atop the North Dallas corridor of information-based industries, the college—and particularly its Learning Resources Center—incorporates new technologies that support the active-learning philosophy.

A library computer system integrates functions on all campuses and provides public-access catalogue terminals throughout the library by using the college's microwave system. In the future, teaching and nonteaching faculty, as well as college and local high school students, will have access to the library data base through personal computers networked to the library's mainframe computer. The Learning Resources Center also offers multiple types of experiential classrooms, two learning theaters, a microcomputer classroom, a closed-circuit television system for individual study stations, and a center for alternative learning that uses media-based instruction.

Having had the opportunity—unusual in the 1980s—for a fresh beginning, the college has taken the best educational theory and practice of the past and the most effective technologies of the present to build a reputation for outstanding instruction, with a focus on active experiential learning in both classroom and library.

New Directions for Community Colleges, no. 71, Fall 1990 © Jossey-Bass Inc., Publishers

Experiential Learning

The term *experiential learning* signifies hands-on, pragmatic learning, as well as the methodology that facilitates active involvement on the part of the learner. In this chapter, that term and a related one, *active learning*, refer to experience-based learning sponsored by an academic institution and characterized by the learner's participation in the learning process. No longer expected to receive information passively from an authority, learners interact with the sources of information—evaluating, integrating, generalizing, and applying new knowledge. In summary, experiential education is learner- and experience-centered, rather than instructor- or curriculum-centered.

Research indicates that the experiential mode enhances learning, and literature documents many significant outcomes. In their summary of the benefits of experiential learning, Kendall and others (1986) list increased confidence in the higher-order cognitive skills and increased skill in directing one's own learning. Strengthened learner motivation (Sexton and Ungerer, 1975) and long-term retention (Specht, 1985) are additional significant outcomes. One of the most significant results of experiential learning, however, is improved integration of newly acquired knowledge with previous learning

The National Institute of Education's (NIE) Study Group on the Conditions of Excellence in American Higher Education (1984) emphatically confirms the importance of active learning to educational excellence. In fact, the NIE explicitly bases many of its final recommendations regarding necessary conditions for excellence in higher education on "the fact that more learning occurs when students are actively engaged in the learning process" (p. 19).

On the basis of such research, Collin County Community College adopted a philosophy of learner-centered education and determined to integrate active learning into all areas of the curriculum. The Learning Resources Center functions as a key learning tool in this overall focus on learning *how* rather than *what*, by emphasizing inquiry, critical analysis, synthesis, and abstract, logical thinking.

Laboratory Component Across the Curriculum

One of the major decisions in integrating active learning into the curriculum involved establishing a laboratory component in the courses of all disciplines, including liberal arts courses. Laboratory assignments are performed outside the classroom and frequently involve learning experiences in the Learning Resources Center. The specific structure, methods, and content of lab components purposely remain fluid and individualized, according to the needs of the subject area and the creativity of the faculty.

Although not all the following features are common to all the labs, they are characteristic of most:

- Learner-centered and student-directed learning
- Emphasis on problem solving, discovery, and inquiry
- Practical application of course content
- Focus on holistic understanding rather than fact acquisition
- Perception-based rather than theory-based learning
- Emphasis on heuristic processes (learning about learning).

American History Lab. An American history lab component illustrates many of the experiential features that characterize lab components across the curriculum. Like many other labs, this one is held primarily in the Learning Resources Center and requires the student to develop a video presentation with accompanying commentary, as well as a research paper based on personal investigation and review of historical film clips.

The method and content of the assignment are only loosely specified by the instructor. Directing his or her own learning, the student determines the focus, scheduling, presentation format, and development of the project. Choosing from a list of broad topics (such as human rights in the 1980s), the student examines the historical events of the period, determines which information is relevant, and generalizes on the significance of events and ideas.

To support this kind of direct learning experience for students and community patrons, LRC staff have purchased numerous materials, as well as editing rights to the *Video Encyclopedia of the Twentieth Century.* This tool contains thousands of film clips from contemporary historical and cultural events, permitting access in either videocassette or videodisc format and affording students the rare opportunity to observe primary historical events, free of commentary or interpretation, and generalize about the significance of the raw data for themselves.

During much of the lab, students learn through visual and oral perception as they study, interpret, and edit video images. While completing their projects, they solve problems, discover answers, and use high-level thinking skills to evaluate, determine relationships of parts to the whole, and conceptualize overall trends and meanings. In this way, the lab promotes holistic understanding, rather than simple mastery of facts. Finally, the lab provides an opportunity for students to discuss the heuristic or cognitive processes they have experienced.

Lab Guidelines and Manuals. The majority of the lab components that the college has developed exhibit some or all of these experiential features. To implement the labs easily and in a manner that encourages risk taking, the college has established minimal guidelines. For each three-hour semester course, students complete an average of one hour of lab work, in addition to three hours of classroom work. Although they receive only the normal three hours of credit, students understand that the experiential lab is an essential, integral part of the course. Moreover, while the college strongly encourages instructors to include experiential learning labs in all courses, they are allowed complete freedom to develop the components.

Teaching faculty have developed laboratory manuals for certain courses to ensure consistent, competency-based experiences throughout the discipline. In the freshman composition course, for instance, instructors have designed a lab manual for all classes. It contains sequential exercises designed to engage students in active learning, and approximately one-third involve learning activities in areas of the Learning Resources Center.

Role of the LRC

The inevitable consequence of learner-centered education that focuses on *how* rather than on *what* is an increasingly active instructional role for the Learning Resources Center. Long before the college library had books on the shelves or students in the stacks, the library faculty and staff clearly understood their role in the learning process. One of the major goals of the college is to assist students in gaining competence in inquiry. Only the initial step in learning to inquire for oneself occurs in the classroom; most of the process involves the LRC.

The role of the LRC staff is to assist students by encouraging and guiding them as they proceed through the steps of inquiry. In all public services, such as reference, alternative learning, and bibliographic instruction, the role of the LRC staff is to help students discover, evaluate, judge, and solve problems.

The instructional function of the library and the focus on experiential learning are particularly evident in bibliographic instruction. Here, the aim is to guide researchers through the various processes involved in inquiry, including formulation and execution of logical research strategies and analysis and evaluation of information. As Bechtel (1986, p. 223) succinctly states, "The proper task of bibliographic instruction becomes teaching critical thinking and enabling participation in intellectual inquiry." Through bibliographic instruction, students learn to understand and master the processes of inquiry. In other words, they learn how to learn for themselves, one of the most important goals of the college.

Role of the Alternative Learning Center

The Alternative Learning Center (ALC) is an area of the LRC specifically designed to facilitate experiential learning and hands-on practice through the use of educational technology. This cross-disciplinary facility serves a diversity of individual learning and teaching styles. It is equipped with a local-area network of IBM PCs, Apple IIGSs, and MacIntosh micro-computers, along with appropriate software. Computer-assisted instruction (CAI) is available for instructors who wish to develop their own computer-ized learning modules. In addition, students, other members of the college community, and local residents may use the ALC to view and edit video-tapes and use computers to create art and generate synthesized music. Interactive videodisc programs, filmstrips, and slide-tape programs are also available in the ALC.

This is not to say that ALC staff are concerned only with hardware and software. They strive toward a balanced view of their role as facilitators of improved instruction. They have adopted the following broad definition of *educational technology* formulated by the Association for Educational Com-munications and Technology (1977, p. 1): "A complex, integrated process, involving people, procedures, ideas, devices, and organization, for analyz-ing problems and devising, implementing, evaluating, and managing solu-tions to those problems involved in all aspects of human learning." As a result of this systems approach to educational technology, the college selects ALC staff primarily on the basis of their teaching abilities and interpersonal skills, placing a strong but secondary emphasis on their expertise in various instructional technologies. The principles discussed by Chickering and Gamson (1987) serve as guidelines for ALC staff, who encourage student-faculty contact, encourage cooperation among students, encourage active learning, give prompt feedback, emphasize time on task, communicate high expectations, and respect diverse talents and ways of learning.

Use of Computers and Other Technology in the ALC

One of the most important roles of the ALC staff is to help instructors who wish to use computers, videotapes, videodiscs, and other hardware and software in the lab components of their courses. CAI offers many opportu-nities for experiential learning that might otherwise be unavailable because of costs, safety factors, or inconvenience.

Students enrolled in United States government courses, for example, work through a legislative-process simulation program, in which they assume the role of congressional representatives. The program requires students not only to know and understand important legislative terms but also to think through the various political problems they encounter. Should the representative compromise on an issue about which the majority of his or her constituents have very strong feelings? An unwise decision will result in the representative's being voted out at the next election.

Other computer simulations offered in the ALC include various types of court trials, historical expeditions, and business strategies and various experiments in psychology, biology, and chemistry. By using the computer, a biology student can "produce" hundreds of generations of fruit flies and can study the probabilities of genetic inheritance and mutation patterns. Tutorials, drill and practice, and other preprogrammed computer packages are also available in virtually every subject area.

In essence, the ALC staff recognizes that the computer's greatest potential for improving instruction rests in its use as an interactive tool for open-ended exploration. Selection of high-quality exploratory software and full use of an instructional computer network work toward that end.

Instructors have access to the network from their offices and can preview software, make assignments, check students' work, and participate in ongoing bulletin-board discussions with colleagues and students. In the future, modem pooling, for accessing various on-line services and providing access to computer resources from students' and faculty members' homes and other remote sites, will also be available.

Telecourses

In addition to promoting the goal of improving instruction in all disciplines, the ALC staff also strives to promote effective use of telecommunications technology in ways that make active-learning experiences accessible to more people. Telecourses that include significant experiential learning are a good example. All telecourses are coordinated and made available through the ALC. Twelve fully transferable credit courses are broadcast throughout the college's service area. After enrolling in the normal manner, telecourse students view the lessons at home or in the ALC, at their convenience. They may also choose to take the courses in a self-paced mode, using ALC facilities.

ALC's "Connections: An Adventure in Learning"

"Connections: An Adventure in Learning" is a series of experiential learning events that are cross-disciplinary and do not rely on technology for their implementation. This program is designed to provide instructors of various disciplines with speakers, films, panel discussions, field trips, debates, performances, and so on, which can be used as lab components across the curriculum.

A recent series on AIDS was used by instructors of English, sociology, biology, psychology, and other disciplines. Other "Connections" programs have focused on substance abuse, the information age, mental health issues, UFOs, the Constitution, and the relationship between art and nature. Because these programs receive prominent coverage from the local news media, they also provide information to staff of local agencies and to residents who attend the sessions.

While accomplishing the dual objectives of making experiential learning more accessible to students and improving instruction in general, ALC staff hope that the LRC/ALC may become a center of exploration and research into cognitive systems, learning models, instructional design, curriculum development and enhancement, educational technology applications, and educational innovation—in short, a center for the improvement of instruction.

Active Learning Throughout the LRC

The ALC demonstrates the participatory nature of the learning activities that take place throughout the Learning Resources Center, using traditional and audiovisual as well as computing resources. Whatever format is used, LRC staff actively guide or instruct students according to their needs as they complete a broad spectrum of active-learning assignments—from research papers (in which students evaluate their sources and discuss the cognitive processes they experienced while doing research) to practical applications of data-base principles (through such projects as setting up a reserved-book data base or designing computer simulations).

One interesting and desirable outcome of lab components such as these is the blurring of the teacher and learner roles. In completing some lab projects, a student may assume the role of instructor, presenting course content to the rest of the class through a video or informational speech. In fact, an increasing number of hands-on lab assignments conclude with students sharing their insights and competence in video presentations. To encourage experimentation in this area and facilitate the showing of students' video projects to other classes and to the entire college, the LRC has designed two learning theaters in the library, Bijou I and Bijou II. They feature flashing, lighted signs and offer continuous showings of student-produced videos and instructional and feature films.

Summary

The LRC at Collin County Community College is the hub of the experiential learning and teaching emphasized at the institution. Staff have chosen resources and technologies and designed facilities to help students with lab projects that require them to discover, evaluate, judge, solve problems, and inquire. Given the continuing dedication of the institution to such student-directed learning and the exciting developments in informational and educational technologies, the central instructional role of the LRC will continue to evolve and expand.

References

Association for Educational Communications and Technology. *The Definition of Educational Technology*. Washington, D.C.: Association for Educational Communications and Technology, 1977.

Bechtel, J. M. "Conversation: A New Paradigm for Librarianship?" *College & Research Libraries*, 1986, 47 (3), 219-229.

Chickering, A. W., and Gamson, Z. F. "Seven Principles for Good Practice in Undergraduate Education." *AAHE Bulletin*, 1987, 39 (7), 3-7.

Kendall, J. C., Duley, J. S., Little, T. C., Permaul, J. S., and Rubin, S. (eds.). *Strengthening Experiential Education Within Your Institution.* Raleigh, N.C.: National Society for Internships and Experiential Education, 1986. 165 pp. (ED 271 055)

Sexton, R. F., and Ungerer, R. A. *Rationales for Experiential Education.* Washington, D.C.: American Association for Higher Education, 1975.

Specht, P. H. "Experiential Learning-Based Versus Lecture-Based Discussion: The Impact of Degree of Participation and Student Characteristics on Comprehension and Retention." *Journal of Business Education*, 1985, 60 (7), 283-287.

Study Group on the Conditions of Excellence in American Higher Education. *Involvement in Learning: Realizing the Potential of American Higher Education.* Washington, D.C.: National Institute of Education, 1984. 127 pp. (ED 246 833)

Richard L. Ducote is dean of the Learning Resources Center at Collin County Community College, McKinney, Texas.

As a reference librarian, Alicia T. Tibbals directs bibliographic instruction at Collin County Community College.

Steven E. Prouty is director of the Alternative Learning Center at Collin County Community College.

The LRC is the logical place in the community college for linking
faculty and students with microcomputer-based learning technology.

LRC Microcomputer Services for Instructional Support

Michael D. Rusk

The microcomputer serves an acknowledged, evolving function at all levels and in all facets of education. Unlike other instructional equipment, microcomputers support a broad spectrum of activities, from producing memos and spreadsheets to downloading the formatted results of on-line searches. Indeed, the potential for microcomputer applications has scarcely been tapped, even while librarians struggle to keep pace with changes that the technology has already made in their learning resources programs.

The LRC is the most accessible and appropriate place on two-year college campuses in which to implement microcomputer applications. LRCs usually have central locations, long hours, and a wide variety of resources and services to support myriad programs and teaching techniques. Many LRCs employ instructional technologists who can assist instructors with software development or modification. LRC staff members generally are service-oriented and familiar with a variety of hardware and software. Having traditionally provided centralized control for instructional resources and equipment, the LRC can serve as a logical clearinghouse for collegewide acquisition and circulation of microcomputer hardware and software.

Furthermore, by its very nature, the LRC provides an atmosphere conducive to experimentation and the use of new technology in authentic situations by faculty and students. The LRC is the only area on campus that provides a large matrix of technological tools, in which the microcomputer is but a single element. Faculty who have benefited by using video programs in their classes tend to be the most amenable to working with LRC staff in developing computer tutorials for their students and in encouraging their colleagues to introduce automated instructional aids in their classes.

Microcomputers in the LRC

Carter (1984) outlines the wide variety of microcomputer user services and library-management functions commonly provided in community college libraries and LRCs. The potential for LRC involvement has now expanded in a number of ways.

Microlabs. LRCs that initially have set up open-access labs without teaching support frequently have found faculty assigning class projects in the labs or users having difficulty with some software applications. As a result, many such LRCs have changed from open labs to classrooms. Micro-computers are networked for group instruction, with applications software and an automated management program stored on a hard disk with a file server.

Microcomputer-Assisted Instruction. The earliest forms of computer-assisted instruction (CAI) employed a number of terminals clustered around a minicomputer, which had enough internal memory and disk space to allow multiuser access to a fixed set of programs. Although students achieved some success with this form of drill-and-practice instruction, the level of interaction was low, while the frustration it caused to instructors was high.

These early systems are now being phased out and replaced in LRC labs with either stand-alone or networked microcomputers, which feature a wide range of software applications supporting instruction, not only in the traditional fields of computer science and engineering but also in the humanities and social sciences. An example of this is the MicroTICCIT system being utilized by Northern Virginia Community College's Alexandria campus and by three other large community college districts (Terwilliger, 1988).

MicroTICCIT is a local-area network system, which at the Alexandria campus LRC supports one hundred student workstations and a user-friendly, course-authoring system for faculty. Alexandria campus faculty have developed and revised complete courses and modules in mathematics, grammar, logic, physics, chemistry, biology, writing, and music. "Master teachers" offer these on a credit basis, having found that students are more likely to complete the modules if the latter are an integral part of the curriculum than if they are available merely as an adjunct.

Some two-year vocational/technical centers, such as the one at Itawamba Community College (Mississippi), are attacking workplace illiteracy with IBM PALS (Principle of the Alphabet Literacy System), which utilizes networked IBM PCs with InfoWindow Displays and videodisc players (Cross, 1989). Nancy Niles, assistant librarian at SUNY's Cobleskill campus, produced a CAI library skills tutorial for the PC with "Trainer-Turned-Author," an authoring system by Raster Technologies. She has made this available to other librarians, who are free to revise it. Nevertheless, the level of student-program interaction in much current CAI is still lower than expected, and such writers as Bozeman and House (1988, p. 88) report continued faculty frustration: "A few teachers will realize substantial benefits, primarily through their own diligence and perseverance, but many others will either avoid involvement altogether or become disenchanted in a short time and then find ways to avoid the technology."

With steadily improving memory and graphic capabilities in microcomputers, CAI programs will become more powerful, elegant, and interactive. LRC CAI will offer greater interaction for students by utilizing videodisc-based programming or hypertext capabilities, which permit movement between text and graphics. The microcomputer center director at Pima Community College has designed an interactive, Hypercard-based library orientation and instruction program, which can be used anywhere on campus. Users can access it for basic information about LRC locations or procedures, or they can go directly to a sequence describing a generic search strategy to use for term papers. "Buttons" on this section will later let students branch off to explanations of how to conduct research in specific subject fields.

Many faculty members require technical assistance in using microcomputer technology and electronic media in their teaching. LRC staff can provide this support in such traditional ways as reviewing, indexing, circulating, and inventorying hardware and software, or in more sophisticated ways, such as designing software, programming, setting up hardware configurations, and planning networks. Moreover, now that many LRCs are supporting instruction with other types of advanced technology (such as satellite dishes, which receive teleconferences in one-way video, two-way audio formats, or telefacsimile machines, which permit document delivery via voice-grade phone lines), LRC staff must fit microcomputers appropriately into the available continuum of technology for LRC instructional support. Librarians may be the first to introduce new programs and devices to faculty, who in turn spread their use throughout the institution. To do this successfully, however, LRC planners must make crucial investments in staff development.

Microliteracy for LRC Staff. Each of the three campuses of Tulsa Junior College (TJC) houses a learning resource center. The print collections of the LRCs number 90,000 volumes; the audiovisual collections emphasize videotapes. The Metro and Southeast campuses are equipped with closed-circuit video delivery. A C-band satellite dish provides teleconferencing services at the Northeast campus. Each LRC utilizes telefacsimile equipment. Some LRC functions, such as video production and technical services, are centralized at one campus, but the college maintains a systems concept for the LRC, shifting resources and staff as service needs change.

Microliteracy for LRC staff became essential in 1983, when TJC established independent, IBM PC–based microcomputing labs on each campus and the LRCs acquired Apple IIs for student use and began conducting online reference searches using IBM PCs with modems. As microcomputer use accelerated throughout the college, LRC staff developed an intensive training program, which focuses on applications used daily in the labs and the LRC. "Microliteracy for Librarians" was initially conceived as a training program for LRC public service staff, but requests for TJC to offer it as a credit class poured in from local public and academic libraries and regional consortia. The team-taught credit course that was developed introduces basic computer concepts and terminology and provides hands-on training in word processing and data management (Rusk and Siddons, 1985).

Similar microliteracy efforts for library staff and instructional faculty have been reported at other community colleges and universities (Piele, Pryor, and Tuckett, 1986). The increased use of microcomputers for accessing information has given librarians opportunities for taking a leadership role in promoting microcomputer and information literacy across campuses and in providing intensive, practical training in the use of new information technology.

Software Collections. To make microcomputer software accessible in the LRC, staff must index it, keep track of all supporting hardware and software documentation, and retain the programs on floppy or hard disk, cassette tape, and (perhaps in the future) on CD-ROM. This provides new challenges for staff in community college technical services (Manes, 1985). Lessons that LRC staff have learned in housing and circulating audiocassettes and videocassettes have been applied to microcomputer software.

A survey of software acquisition and control in Michigan community college libraries and other academic libraries (Doyle and Bosler, 1985) indicated high levels of use of microcomputers by students and faculty but low levels of LRC staff involvement in helping instructors develop microcomputer-related class assignments. LRCs also tended to maintain close control over commercially produced curriculum-support or library-management software, because of stringent copyright restrictions.

LRC microlabs can comply with copyright regulations by purchasing enough copies of a single program to meet the anticipated demand and then restricting simultaneous use of the program to the number of copies owned. Students who use the open-access lab in the LRC at SUNY's Cobleskill campus must first complete a brief orientation on lab operations and sign a copyright-compliance agreement, which is kept on file for six years, a procedure that cleared the LRC of liability when the FBI prosecuted a student for appropriating software for commercial purposes (Carter, personal communication, 1989). Although the American Library Association and the distributors of children's games appear to have negotiated the exemption of nonprofit libraries from restrictions inherent in the proposed Computer Software Rental Amendments Act, it is not clear whether academic libraries will fit into this category. National associations need to inform Congress about the needs of higher education regarding microcomputer software.

Assistance with Interactive Authoring Systems. Perhaps the most exciting new service the LRC can offer, once microcomputer activities have spread collegewide, is to help faculty create or modify software. Instructional software can be created from scratch with a programming language (such as BASIC), but the process is much more time-consuming than using an authoring system, and it obviously requires staff with high-level programming skills.

Authoring systems are computer programs that permit a user to construct other programs. The creation of instructional programs requires a *content* specialist (an educator with a concept to be developed) and a *technical* specialist (a programmer who can translate the concept into program form). An appropriately staffed LRC can provide assistance with authoring microcomputer software, but sound instructional techniques must provide the basis. Programming specialists must rely on faculty members to invest considerable time and skill in developing the logic and content of each program they produce. Too much current courseware has been developed by programmers who have no training in cognitive processes or instructional design. Gibbons (1987), anticipating expert systems of the future, warns against permitting programmers or systems analysts to set the rules of computer tutoring and challenges instructional designers to become involved in the process.

As microcomputers grow more powerful, they will make it possible for staff to create "intelligent" software, such as the program that the University of Virginia teacher training department is using, which simulates student interactions (Strang and Loper, 1986). The MacIntosh Hypercard offers exciting possibilities for developing branching instructional programs that use CDs and interactive videodisc.

Selection of Software and Hardware. LRCs can serve as coordinating units for the selection, acquisition, circulation, maintenance, and control of campus software and hardware. LRC staff can prevent unnecessary duplication and provide evaluations of hardware and software through microcomputer journals and various on-line data bases, such as DIALOG's Business Software Database (Information Sources, Inc.), MENU, International Software Database (Black Box Corporation), Microcomputer Index (Learned Information, Inc.), Micro Software Directory—SOFT (Online, Inc.), and Microcomputer Software Guide (R. R. Bowker Company). Librarians can also direct faculty and students to microcomputer user groups, which tend now to be organized more around software packages than around hardware.

Software Clearinghouses. The diversity of in-house software development projects under way in higher education has led some authors (for example, Danielson, 1987) to predict that the next generation of instructional microcomputer software will be designed in classrooms and laboratories. One challenge for community college LRC staff in the 1990s will be to encourage the sharing of locally developed software among and within institutions. Telecommunications makes this possible, and the LRC is the ideal agency to coordinate this activity. A number of such networks and clearinghouses currently exist.

Tulsa Junior College recently received Kellogg Foundation funding to establish a center for coordinating electronic communication among librarians, faculty, and programmers and to promote the development and sharing of instructional courseware among state colleges and universities. TJC is developing microcomputer software and high-quality computer graphic images and gathering and indexing these materials, together with programs provided by other institutions, in a master data base. Users can access this data base through an electronic bulletin board, which permits them to download holdings and access a quarterly newsletter, *LINKED* (Rusk, 1989).

A similar project is in place at Johnson County Community College (Kansas), where a system called the Community College IBM Information Sharing System (CCIIS) uses a data base and electronic bulletin board (ISAAC) to make educators across the nation aware of courseware development projects that may be of common interest. SUNY's Cobleskill campus LRC maintains a data base of campus-owned software and can locate all types of software and audiovisual material available in New York through a clearinghouse created by the SUNY librarians' association.

Wisc-Ware, established by the Academic Computing Center of the University of Wisconsin (Madison), is a primary distributor of the latest research-and-instruction software available for MS DOS–based microcomputers. The center will provide a free membership guide for those who call 1-800-543-3201.

CD-ROM and the Automated Reference Center. Many LRCs provide microcomputer workstations that give patrons access to popular CD-ROM data bases. Some of these CD-ROM products give users automatic on-line access to the most current citations, while others provide the full text of cited articles. Fitzwater and Fradkin (1988) report several grant-funded innovations that use standard types of equipment and telecommunications packages that permit institutions to share a variety of CD-ROM products through telefax (with Grammafax software). They have also experimented with a similar system, which can give users at remote sites dial access (through PC Anywhere) to the college's CD-ROM data bases.

The LRC at SUNY's Cobleskill campus is one of many that have designed automated reference centers after the prototype established at the University of Vermont (Eaton, 1987). These separate areas in the LRC house microcomputer workstations that permit direct user searching of both CD-ROM and "after dark" on-line data bases. Automated reference centers permit staff to provide group or computer-assisted instruction in menu-aided on-line searching and to make cost comparisons among different types of products and searching techniques.

Automated Integrated Library Systems. Many LRCs in larger community college systems have acquired minicomputer-based turnkey systems, which provide modules for acquisitions, circulation, serials control, media scheduling, inventory, management reports, and an on-line public catalogue. All community colleges in Florida will soon be networked on such a system. In smaller community colleges, however, librarians have been patiently waiting for the prices of automated systems to drop. According to Walton and Bridge (1989), prices have stayed high because of continuing high costs for software licenses and support, system installation, and staff training, but these authors predict growing interest among vendors in systems for smaller libraries: with "power and disk storage doubling every two years (per technology dollar invested), it is only a matter of time before . . . microcomputer-based library systems will be able to provide suitable power to support the terminal loads and transaction throughput, along with adequate storage for and . . . ability to load, maintain, and output MARC records" (pp. 42–43).

Conclusion

Increased microcomputer power should mean greater instructional power, alternative teaching strategies, more effective support services, and enhanced learning. LRC planners will have to decide whether to purchase a few expensive microcomputers, with large amounts of memory, powerful graphic monitors, and networking capability, or to acquire larger numbers of less powerful microcomputers, which can serve more students simultaneously. Regardless of the approach, today's students must have access to microcomputers, not only for learning the content in many disciplines but also for carrying out the work. For instance, accounting students and those in all design fields now require skills in computer graphics (Slayton, 1988).

Because new technology, such as CD-ROM and interactive video, is expensive, some LRCs may become technologically elite, while others will struggle to provide basic services. Telecommunications links for sharing materials (such as CD-ROMs or in-house–developed software) can help narrow this gap.

This has been the decade of the microcomputer in community college LRC programs. As the technology evolves, however, it must be viewed as only one element of the instructional technology matrix of the LRC, although a highly flexible one. Microcomputer-based products, such as the MINDSET Videographics System, make possible the special visual effects that in the recent past were possible only with sophisticated equipment that exceeded the budgets of most programs. Optical disk technology will allow faculty and students to easily access large amounts of information, text, video, and other visual materials through microcomputers. New curricula, such as desktop publishing and graphic programming, will utilize the graphics capabilities of the new generation of microcomputers, and computer animation and 3-D graphics will soon appear in simulation software for instruction.

The proposed new standards for two-year-college LRCs recognize the centrality of the microcomputer to LRC services, noting that it permits networking and resource sharing; timely, enhanced, and expanded access to information; and the transmission of basic skills.

In summary, both the microcomputer and the LRC provide support for all units of the college, the LRC serving as the appropriate campus unit to link microcomputer capabilities with the community college instructional program.

References

Bozeman, W. C., and House, J. E. "Microcomputers in Education: The Second Generation." *T.H.E. Journal*, 1988, *15* (6), 88.

Carter, E. M. "Applications of Microcomputers in Libraries and Learning Resource Centers." In D. A. Dellow and L. H. Poole (eds.), *Microcomputer Applications in Administration and Instruction.* New Directions for Community Colleges, no. 47. San Francisco: Jossey-Bass, 1984.

Cross, C. "IBM Looks to Community College Programs to Rescue American Economy." *Community College Week*, 1989, *1* (15), 9.

Danielson, W. "The Next Generation of Academic Microcomputer Software." *Perspectives in Computing*, 1987, *7* (2), 37.

Doyle, J. M., and Bosler, G. F. "Microcomputer Software Acquisition and Control: A Survey of Selected Michigan Libraries." *Community & Junior College Libraries*, 1985, *4* (1), 53–66.

Eaton, N. L. "Integrating Electronic Information Systems into the Reference Services Budget." *Reference Librarian*, 1987, *19*, 161–177.

Fitzwater, D., and Fradkin, B. "CD-ROM + Fax = Shared Reference Resource." *American Libraries*, 1988, *19* (5), 385.

Gibbons, A. S. "Instructional Technologists Must Play a Stronger Role in AI Development." *Instructional Delivery Systems*, 1987, *1* (5), 12–16.

Manes, L. "Much Ado About Micro Software." *Community & Junior College Libraries*, 1985, *3* (4), 45–52.

Piele, L. J., Pryor, J., and Tuckett, H. W. "Teaching Microcomputer Literacy: New Roles for Academic Librarians." *College & Research Libraries*, 1986, *47* (4), 374–378.

Rusk, M. D. "Courseware Development Center: Electronic Sharing of Instructional Software." *Community & Junior College Libraries*, 1989, *6* (2), 1–7.

Rusk, M., and Siddons, J. "Microliteracy for Librarians." *Community & Junior College Libraries*, 1985, 3 (4), 45–52.

Slayton, J. "Toward a New Media Technology." *T.H.E. Journal*, 1988, 15 (6), 87–89.

Strang, J., and Loper, A. "Microcomputer Support for Teacher-Pupil Dialogue." *Journal of Educational Technology Systems*, 1986, 14 (2), 85–86, 119–128.

Terwilliger, G. "TICCIT—Instructional Technology's Best-Kept Secret." *Community & Junior College Libraries*, 1988, 6 (1), 45–54.

Walton, R. A., and Bridge, F. R. "Automated System Marketplace, 1988: Focused on Fulfilling Commitments." *Library Journal*, 1989, 114 (6), 41–52.

Michael D. Rusk is dean of learning resources centers, Tulsa Junior College.

The LRC must evaluate its role in the institution's instructional program with respect to accreditation criteria, public calls for program assessment, and professional concerns about standards and performance/outcomes measures.

Self-Study Methods for the Library and the LRC

Antoinette M. Kania

In the 1980s, state authorities, accreditors, and taxpayers challenged public higher education to demonstrate, in a measurable and credible way, that it is providing the kinds of programs and services that are worthy of financial support and public trust. These calls for more accountability and assessment have grown out of a widespread concern for the general decline in quality and rise in cost of the educational enterprise. Evidence indicates that students are graduating from college without basic knowledge and intellectual skills, that there has been a continuing decline in overall efficiency and productivity, and that leaders may be unwilling or unable to identify and solve these problems (Ewell, 1987; Finn, 1988; Moore, 1986; Spangehl, 1988).

Need for an LRC Assessment Model

The assessment movement has gained public attention, and few institutions have escaped its impact. Ewell (1987, p. 24) found eleven states that had "addressed assessment as a matter of policy and statute." No two state mandates were alike, however, and little direction or assistance with assessment models appeared to be forthcoming.

Ewell and Boyer (1988, p. 46), in a follow-up report, found that colleges that "had adopted a proactive stance" in response to the mandates were in a far better position to influence the substance and direction of their own assessment than were those that waited passively for objectives and prototypes to be developed by the state or others. Ewell and Boyer urge institutions to take the initiative in designing their own assessment

NEW DIRECTIONS FOR COMMUNITY COLLEGES, no. 71, Fall 1990 © Jossey-Bass Inc., Publishers

models, since college officials ought to be the experts on whom legislatures rely for appropriate and acceptable models and standards. Thus, knowledge and use of assessment models and methods are the key.

LRC's Role in Institutional Assessment and Accreditation. Breivik (1987, p. 44) warns that within this environment of educational reform the search for academic quality "should not go forward without [examination of] the role of libraries." Institutions will expect their libraries and LRCs to provide evidence that their programs and services are producing effective results, with a level of demonstrated quality that consistently meets the needs of users, not only for purposes of accountability but also for accreditation, improvement, and planning.

The impact of an accreditation review is felt not only at the institutional level but also, for the learning resources center, at the departmental or program level. At this level, in particular, very little improvement-oriented evaluation and analysis have occurred, and the greatest need for guidance exists (Kells, 1983). That evaluation of academic libraries for accreditation is likely to be an agenda item for the future was reinforced by E. K. Fretwell, Jr., who has stated his intention, as the new chair of the Council on Postsecondary Education, to ask regional accreditation agencies to "highlight evaluation of campus libraries and their use" as part of the evaluation and self-study process for institutional accreditation (cited in Breivik, 1987, p. 46).

For the LRC, assessment also needs to be considered a critical component of the planning cycle, where the results of an activity or a service should be analyzed in light of originally stated goals. Moreover, the primary purpose of assessment—to effect change and bring about improvement—is an outgrowth of the planning process. It is this assessment component that institutions and their LRCs do least well, at least in terms of any meaningful and systematic method (Casserly, 1987).

Of particular interest, in this regard, is the recent move in Pennsylvania's state system of higher education to mandate academic program review that includes libraries. This 1987 initiative requires all universities in the system to conduct comprehensive, ongoing program review of all academic departments and support areas on a five-year cycle. The purposes are to contribute to universitywide planning efforts, to enable appropriate responses to accreditation requirements, and to ensure that the quality of the academic programs is being kept as high as possible. University libraries are to be reviewed under this mandate in the same manner and with the same degree of scrutiny as academic departments.

Aids to LRC Assessment Efforts. Recognition of the need to help LRCs conduct useful, outcomes-oriented self-studies linked to goal setting, planning, and performance evaluation has generated several responses from the professional community. In 1985, the Rutgers School of Communication, Information, and Library Studies began sponsoring, as part of its Professional Development Studies program, annual workshops on academic library self-studies. These are an outgrowth of biannual workshops on institutional self-study conducted by H. R. Kells, Rutgers University, and the Middle States Association Commission on Higher Education. Kells and the present author have designed and conducted the current workshops specifically to address systematic self-study at the program (or library/ LRC) level. After long debate and delay, a task force on performance measures of the Association of College and Research Libraries (ACRL) commissioned the writing of a performance-measures manual for academic libraries, similar in concept to Zweizig and Rodger's (1982) widely acclaimed book. In light of all this, this chapter presents a self-study model and case study to illustrate how to apply the self-assessment process in the LRC for the purposes of accountability, accreditation, decision making, or planning.

Self-Study Model for the LRC

This model is based both on the Kells model for programmatic self-study and on findings that concern the use of regional accreditation standards for academic libraries in conjunction with performance measures (Kells, 1983; Kania, 1988b). The Kells model places special emphasis on *design*. Kells maintains that only a well-conceived plan for self-assessment, supported by those in leadership positions, can yield a useful result leading to improvement and change. He offers several models for design, generally based on the data available for analysis at the start of the study and the existing level of institutional planning and research. The less information available and the less ongoing planning conducted by the institution or department, the more comprehensive the self-study needs to be.

The second aspect of the Kells model concerns *organization*, emphasizing the structure and function of group and staff work. Essential organizational elements include use of natural work groups where possible, particularly at the program level; identification of good leaders and appropriate work-group members; and careful sequencing of activities and setting of reasonable timetables.

The third aspect involves *group work*: holding broad-based discussions, collecting additional data, drawing conclusions, and drafting recommendations with timetables. Kells stresses the importance, during this phase, of acting on some of these recommendations before completing the self-study. Prior action on recommendations lends credibility to the evaluation effort, both for local cynics and for external review groups.

During *implementation*—the fourth aspect and end of the cycle—the institution widely distributes the final report. If an external team visits and augments or supports the study's recommendations, a follow-up process is established for monitoring progress toward addressing those recommendations.

The following model combines the Kells model with a process that uses standards, criterion levels for achievement in the local setting, and performance measures to assess the degree of achievement.

Use of Academic Library Standards. To date, academic library standards have not been very useful in guiding self-study for accreditation or other evaluation purposes. Those that are qualitative (such as those in major portions of the ACRL professional and regional accreditation standards) are too broad and general to be of any practical use. Those that are quantitative (such as the formulas for size of collections, staff, and facilities in the ACRL professional and many specialized accreditation standards) are too prescriptive and fail to consider local circumstances. None set priorities, nor are any of them outcomes-oriented or based on research.

A recent model set of qualitative standards, developed from existing regional accreditation standards, is based on research from the field, incorporates priorities for degree of recommended achievement, is outcomes-oriented, and provides assistance for outcomes assessment by identifying performance measures that are easy and practical to apply (Kania, 1988a).

At about the time this model set was being published, the June 1988 draft revision of the 1979 *Standards for University Libraries* was proposed for review by the Association of Research Libraries and ACRL, and it proved to be the first set of professional association standards to focus on both outcomes and performance evaluation. Recognizing that each university library has unique surroundings and circumstances, these standards recommend that each one determine its own criteria for performance and evaluation. The revised standards also set forth a self-evaluation process that includes systematic examination of mission, development of measurable goals and objectives, and assessment of how well stated goals have been met according to appropriate performance measures. While the revised standards are noteworthy in these respects, they fall short of providing assistance with the last step in the process: identifying performance measures.

Use of Performance Measures. Many in the profession have advocated delaying improvements in the standards until more research has been done to replicate and refine existing measures, but this stance is no longer feasible in our era of accountability. Moreover, as long as ten years ago, DuMont and DuMont (1979) were maintaining that although there was a need to test and refine existing techniques, enough methods existed even then to assess the effectiveness of libraries. Even so, Turner (1988, p. 2) reports considerable reluctance on the part of librarians to use performance measures; some apparently feel threatened, while others "would rather measure miles of shelves than the efficiency of the reference desk or the circulation per student." Turner also acknowledges, however, that others have responded to the changing environment by setting performance standards to assist them in competing for scarce resources on their campuses.

There exists a substantial collection of performance measures for evaluating LRCs, as well as documentation for identifying those that are appropriate and practical to employ. Tested methods are also available for evaluating collections, library use, reference services, and document availability (Christiansen, Davis, and Reed-Scott, 1983; Hall, 1985; Kania, 1988b; Mansbridge, 1986; Von Seggern, 1987).

In the following case study, an LRC of a hypothetical community college conducts a self-study as part of the institution's accreditation process. The study describes the LRC's relationship to the collegewide self-study process and the way its subcommittee adapts existing standards and selects local criterion levels of performance, selects and implements performance measures, sets a timetable and allocates human and fiscal resources to carry out the self-study, and makes recommendations for improvement.

Case Study: The LRC's Relationship to the Collegewide Self-Study

Lawrence Community College is a medium-sized public two-year college in the Northeast. It has a full- and part-time enrollment of 11,500 and a full-time faculty of 246. It offers associate degrees in the liberal arts and sciences and in a number of vocational/technical areas, including business, allied health, automotive technology, graphic design, and hotel/restaurant management.

In slightly under two years, Lawrence will be visited for reaccreditation by its regional association, and so the president has appointed a college-wide steering committee to design and implement the institutional self-study. The committee has recommended that the scope of the self-study be comprehensive and has formulated a subcommittee structure, which includes one for the LRC. The LRC associate director of public and technical services, who serves as the LRC's representative to the collegewide steering committee, has been asked to chair the LRC subcommittee, which is to consist of nine members selected from the LRC staff, the classroom faculty, and the student body.

The LRC has ten professional staff, including the director, the associate director of public and technical services, and the associate director of instructional media services. It is organized into four major departments: readers' services (reference, on-line searching, and bibliographic instruction), access services (circulation, reserve, and interlibrary loan), technical services (cataloguing, acquisitions, collection development, and serials), and instructional media services (graphics, photography, and audiovisual/ video production and distribution). Each of these departments has elected a representative to the LRC subcommittee. The library director will not sit on the subcommittee, but she has advocated wholehearted support for the process.

Lawrence's LRC has a collection that includes 102,500 volumes and approximately 750 serials subscriptions. Its total operating budget for the previous year was $1,335,000, including $125,000 for books and periodicals and $19,500 for audiovisual materials. The LRC participates in such automated systems as OCLC (for cataloguing, acquisitions, and interlibrary loan) and DIALOG, BRS, and InfoTrac (for bibliographic searching and reference).

Through the regional accreditation association, the LRC director became aware of an experimental set of academic library standards developed in a research project on accreditation, which suggested performance measures. She recommended that the subcommittee utilize these standards in the LRC self-study, in conjunction with both the regional accreditation and ACRL professional standards. The subcommittee reviewed them in the context of local circumstances. After discussing the standards at the monthly LRC staff meeting, the subcommittee decided that the LRC could benefit most by focusing on three areas: the level of students' and faculty's satisfaction with the LRC's materials and services; utilization of the book collection, overall and by subject areas; and the degree to which books are available when needed. The subcommittee felt the existing data, collected or compiled on a routine basis, would suffice for completing a relatively comprehensive study of the LRC, but appropriate questionnaires or interviews could provide more information if it were needed in some areas.

The subcommittee planned its timetable in March, twenty months before the team visit. Technical Services staff were to conduct the book-use study during the summer, Access Services and Instructional Media staff were to conduct the user survey in October and November, and the Readers' Services staff the book-availability study during the following March and April. Two members of the subcommittee would act as liaisons to these studies. During the interim, the subcommittee planned to analyze the results of the last self-study, draft its report and recommendations for the collegewide committee, and plan the next study.

Book-Use Study. For the book-use study, the subcommittee used the "last circulation date" methodology first described by Trueswell (1976) and later effectively applied by Trochim (1985), whose detailed manual, samples, and worksheets make planning and implementation simple and inexpensive. The method determines book-use patterns of a collection over a specific period by subject, age, and last circulation date of the books. One staff member supervised two available student aides, twenty hours a week during June and July, to collect data on a recommended random sample of 4,100 books. During August, the aides entered data into the central computer, and frequency distributions and cross-tabulations were obtained.

Since literature on the topic reports an average overall usage rate of only 45 percent to 55 percent for college library collections, the subcommittee had set the criterion level at 70 percent, to be achieved over five years. Lawrence's results of 58.7 percent, however, were similar to those reported in the literature. Book use in subject categories often defied staff expectations. For instance, the volume of circulation of materials for business and data processing—programs experiencing rapid growth—was relatively low in comparison with that for books on mathematics. Moreover, fewer than 50 percent of the books in many classifications circulated during this time, and use of those volumes decreased as age of material increased.

The book-use study raised a number of questions regarding the collection's relevance to the curriculum, its lack of currency, its ability to respond to student and faculty needs, and the relationship of the LRC to the instructional programs. Therefore, the subcommittee recommended that faculty members help LRC staff assess the relevance and currency of the collection. Since the study indicated a need for a closer working relationship between librarians and classroom faculty, the LRC made arrangements to have librarians attend at least three meetings of each department each academic year. They also planned to have the academic departments assist in evaluating the collection after the accreditation visit. The subcommittee also expected the other two studies to provide useful information about the collection.

User Survey. The LRC adapted an instrument employed by Budd and DiCarlo (1982) to assess user satisfaction with both library and audiovisual services. Like Budd and DiCarlo, the LRC conducted a pretest of the questionnaire and mailed it to all faculty and to a random sample of 500 students. Since Budd and DiCarlo had been satisfied with an average return rate from faculty of 45.2 percent and from students of 29.1 percent, the subcommittee was pleased with LCC response rates of 48 percent and 37 percent, respectively. Respondents were asked to rate (on a scale of 1 to 7, with 7 the highest) both how important individual services were to them and how well LRC staff carried them out. The LRC staff had set a criterion level of 5 or higher.

Student aides entered data collected during two weeks in October, and staff conducted a simple t test to obtain the performance rating and the statistical significance between the importance of each item and the performance rating. Only 45 percent of the items rated by faculty and 27.6 percent of those rated by students met or exceeded the LCC criterion level. Areas of strength were environmental conditions (such as lighting and cleanliness, although noise and temperature were rated as poor), arrangement and ease of use of the catalogue, and hours of weekly operation.

Faculty rated as good the library staff's reference assistance and willingness to listen and respond to needs. Students' ratings on these same qualities were considerably lower, a finding that may imply preferential treatment of faculty. Problems identified by students were delayed or improper shelving of books, limited weekend hours, poor arrangement of periodicals shelves, malfunctioning equipment, and inadequate reference and book collections.

The LRC subcommittee generated the following recommendations from this study:

- Rearrange periodicals shelving to improve access
- Vary staffing patterns to increase weekend hours on a trial basis
- Evaluate the schedules and performance of student aides
- Methodically train users not to reshelve materials, in order to achieve better stack maintenance
- Review repair and maintenance procedures for audiovisual equipment
- Evaluate the book collection with faculty assistance.

By the time the accreditation team arrived, the following November, LRC staff had started or completed work on all but the last of these recommendations.

Book-Availability Study. Since the literature reports that the average user success rate in finding materials when needed is only about 60 percent, the LRC set its criterion level at a more optimistic 65 percent and utilized a practical method for measuring it, developed by Kantor (1984). During February and March, staff distributed 989 questionnaires and collected 506 usable forms (to achieve an appropriate sample size of 500 and a return rate of 51 percent) in a two-step procedure. Two hours a day, Monday through Friday, one librarian handed out worksheets to students at the card catalogue, asking them to record information about books they needed and could not find listed in the catalogue or found listed in the catalogue and available on the shelf or found listed in the catalogue but not on the shelf. A second librarian then attempted to locate books that students said they could not find and recorded the various reasons why the books could not be located, such as "not owned," "incorrect call number," "misshelved," or "in circulation." Of the 1,750 titles that users searched for, 1,015 (58 percent) were located. Of the 735 (42 percent) not located, 61 (8.3 percent) were in reserve, 82 (11.2 percent) were on the shelves where they were supposed to have been, and 165 (22.5 percent) were actually not available. Almost half the failures (46 percent), therefore, were due to users' errors or failure to understand the system. Of the other 394 unavailable titles, 292 (74 percent) were circulating, 75 (19 percent) were unaccounted for, and 27 (7 percent) were on interlibrary loan, missing in binding, or in some similar category.

The LRC subcommittee made the following recommendations as a result of this study:

- Conduct an inventory of the collection to identify and perhaps replace missing titles

- Make information on reserve books available at the catalogue
- Identify books in high demand and make them more widely available
- Improve bibliographic instruction on locating books.

The LRC scheduled the inventory after the accreditation visit and just before the collection evaluation. They decided that the new, automated library system they were acquiring would identify reserve materials for patrons. Then they reduced the circulation period from six weeks to four, to increase the availability of high-use items; began to study the feasibility of purchasing duplicate copies of selected materials; and created a combined librarian–classroom faculty task force to design a credit course for library research skills.

In summary, LRC staff felt, as a result of the self-study, that they had made significant progress in improving LRC resources and services. They planned a regular cycle of similar studies, to monitor and evaluate their progress on the recommendations of the self-study and to provide ongoing planning to improve the effectiveness of the LRC.

References

Breivik, P. S. "Making the Most of Libraries." *Change,* 1987, *19* (4), 44–52.

Budd, J., and DiCarlo, M. "Measures of User Evaluation at Two Academic Libraries." *Library Research,* 1982, *4* (1), 71–84.

Casserly, M. "Accreditation-Related Self-Study as a Planned Change Process: Factors Relating to Its Success in Academic Libraries." *Journal of Library Administration,* 1987, *8* (1), 85–105.

Christiansen, D. E., Davis, C. R., and Reed-Scott, J. "Guide to Collection Evaluation Through Use and User Studies." *Library Resources and Technical Services,* 1983, *27* (4), 432–440.

DuMont, R. R., and DuMont, P. F. "Measuring Library Effectiveness: A Review and an Assessment." In M. H. Harris (ed.), *Advances in Librarianship.* New York: Academic Press, 1979.

Ewell, P. T. "Assessment: Where Are We?" *Change,* 1987, *19* (1), 23–28.

Ewell, P. T., and Boyer, C. M. "Acting Out State-Mandated Assessment: Evidence from Five States." *Change,* 1988, *20* (4), 41–47.

Finn, C. E. "Judgment Time for Higher Education: In the Court of Public Opinion." *Change,* 1988, *20* (4), 35–39.

Hall, B. H. *Collection Assessment Manual for Colleges and Universities.* Phoenix, Ariz.: Oryx Press, 1985.

Kania, A. M. "Academic Library Standards and Performance Measures." *College & Research Libraries,* 1988a, *49* (1), 16–23.

Kania, A. M. *Performance Measures for Academic Libraries: A Twenty-Year Retrospective.* Selden, N.Y.: Suffolk Community College, 1988b. 8 pp. (ED 293 540)

Kantor, P. B. *Objective Performance Measures for Academic and Research Libraries.* Washington, D.C.: Association of Research Libraries, 1984.

Kells, H. R. *Self-Study Processes: A Guide for Postsecondary Institutions.* (2nd ed.) New York: Macmillan, 1983. 173 pp. (ED 243 387)

Mansbridge, J. "Availability Studies in Libraries." *Library and Information Science Research,* 1986, *8* (10), 299–314.

Moore, K. M. "Assessment of Institutional Effectiveness." In J. Losak (ed.), *Applying Institutional Research in Decision Making.* New Directions for Community Colleges, no. 56. San Francisco: Jossey-Bass, 1986.

Spangehl, S. D. "The Push to Assess." *Change,* 1988, *19* (1), 35–39.

"Standards for University Libraries: Evaluation of Performance (Draft)." *College & Research Libraries News,* 1988, *49* (6), 343–350.

Trochim, M. K. *Measuring the Book Circulation of a Small Academic Library Collection: A Manual.* Washington, D.C.: Association of Research Libraries, 1985. 86 pp. (ED 266 785)

Trueswell, R. W. "Growing Libraries: Who Needs Them? A Statistical Basis for a No-Growth Collection." In D. Gore (ed.), *Farewell to Alexandria.* Westport, Conn.: Greenwood Press, 1976.

Turner, J. A. "Academic Libraries Urged to Study Needs of Users and Set Performance Standards." *Chronicle of Higher Education,* January 27, 1988, p. 5.

Von Seggern, M. "Assessment of Reference Service." *RQ,* 1987, *26* (4), 487–495.

Zweizig, D., and Rodger, E. J. *Output Measures for Public Libraries.* Chicago: American Library Association, 1982.

Antoinette M. Kania is the dean of libraries, Suffolk Community College, State University of New York, Selden.

LRC staffs, within current restrictions, need to initiate and evaluate innovative instruction that accommodates nontraditional students, incorporates new technology, and develops critical-thinking skills.

A Survey of User Education Programs in Community College LRCs

Eileen Dubin

Since World War II, there has been a tremendous growth in United States higher education. This democratization of opportunity has resulted in large numbers of nontraditional students entering colleges and universities. The open-door policy of community colleges in particular has brought in students who do not fit older stereotypes of the average freshman.

To address the needs of all their students, community colleges with comprehensive missions have offered liberal arts and sciences programs to prepare students for four-year colleges and universities or for lifelong learning; vocational and technical programs to provide training, retraining, and upgrading of job skills; and preparatory programs to furnish students with secondary school certification and upgraded academic skills for success in postsecondary education. The increasing enrollment of nontraditional learners, however, has made developmental education the central focus for many rural and urban two-year colleges.

This broad-based community college mission has been in place with only minor changes over the years. Bodi (1988), Breivik (1987), Dale (1988), Dubin and Bigelow (1986), Kerr (1988), Kreider and Walleri (1988), Martell and Ware (1988), and Svinicki and Schwartz (1988) have all stressed the importance of literacy, writing, and conceptual skills and the need to assess programs claiming to nurture these skills. The educational community, including two-year colleges, has responded by examining its performance.

Eaton (1988, p. 4) examines the role of the community college in the educational process and the need for a "framework of values by which the future 'work' of the community college will be organized, understood and sanctioned." She concludes (p. 5) that "the emerging community college profile urges a special commitment to the central role of intellectual inquiry (the teaching-learning experience), to the quality of style of the people needed (the leadership experience) . . . and to the prevailing institutional climate (the culture experience)." Indeed, she claims (p. 17), through clear purpose and meaningful standards of quality, community colleges can "provide a clear agenda of intent for their higher education effort: education for competence, mobility and success."

Development of LRC Bibliographic Instruction

Since the 1960s, there has been an upsurge in library user education in all types of academic libraries. With the assistance of professional organizational guidelines, model statements, and substantial research and writing in the field, librarians have been provided with a conceptual basis for bibliographic instruction (Fjallbrant and Malley, 1984).

In the mid 1970s, there was an emphasis in academic libraries on writing goals and objectives for bibliographic instruction (BI). Teaching materials encompassed self-guided tours, slide-tape presentations, videotapes, handbooks, and printed library guides. Self-guided skills workbooks proved particularly useful in reaching large numbers of undergraduates. Methods of library instruction included introduction through freshman English classes, credit courses, and course-integrated instruction, in which librarians worked closely with faculty members to blend BI into courses.

The changing student body and advances in library technology are again challenging librarians to redefine their instructional role. Hisle (1988) cites disagreement among top community college administrators and LRC directors and deans about the role of the LRC in the instructional program. While college presidents and vice-presidents in his study were optimistic about the possibility of LRCs helping to develop students' learning skills and about having the necessary resources for LRCs to participate in instructional design, LRC directors were dubious about the likelihood that their units would assume such an active role in the college's instructional program. Perhaps the optimism of the administrators reflected a "public relations" approach to responding to Hisle's questionnaire, while the pessimism of the LRC directors may have been based on previous failure to obtain funding for new programs.

National Survey of LRC Services

Late in the spring of 1988, the Community and Junior College Libraries Section of ACRL sent a questionnaire to 1,276 community colleges to assess the state of the art of BI in their LRCs. The 336 questionnaires that were returned came from every state, with the bulk from California, Illinois, Kansas, New York, North Carolina, Ohio, Pennsylvania, South Carolina, and Virginia.

The questionnaire was designed to assess the current role that LRCs play in instruction, the innovative ideas they are testing, and the possibilities that exist for their librarians to forge partnerships with nonlibrary faculty in teaching library skills. The timing of the questionnaire seemed particularly appropriate, since *Building Communities* (American Association of Community and Junior Colleges, 1988) had just been issued, emphasizing the teaching-learning role in the classroom.

Structure of LRCs. To put information about BI and other instructional services into perspective, the questionnaire sought background information on the size of each respondent's institution and the administrative structure, staffing, services, and collections of the LRC. Community college LRCs vary widely in structure and organization. Many include a centralized library, audiovisual delivery, media production, and telecourse distribution. While most LRCs incorporate both print and nonprint materials, some have only print collections.

Lines of authority also vary. In most instances, the director of LRC reports to the college official in charge of academic affairs. Because of the fluidity of organizational patterns, however, that individual may be academic vice-president, dean of instructional services, or (in some instances) a dean, associate dean, or vice-president from outside the academic division (Veit, 1975).

Size and Staffing of LRCs. Sixty-two percent of the schools responding had three thousand or fewer students, and 12 percent had over seven thousand FTEs. The twenty schools (5.4 percent) reporting enrollments of over twelve thousand are multicampus institutions. While all the LRCs have full-time administrators, two-thirds (244) report having only two professionals, indicating that in many colleges the administrator also serves as a librarian. The support staff ranges from two to fifteen, with widely varying levels of student help.

The revised "Standards for Two-Year College Learning Resources Programs" (1989) suggest that colleges with three thousand or fewer FTEs should meet a basic staffing requirement of three professionals and one administrator. Clearly, two-thirds of the colleges responding to this survey do not meet this minimum standard. Most of the larger institutions also fail to meet minimum requirements. Those with enrollments of over twelve thousand average one administrator, seven professionals, one media specialist, and one instructional designer each (see Table 1).

Services. Respondents identified the services provided by their LRCs from the following list:

Central library   TV studio
Audiovisual distribution   Telecourse distribution

Table 1. Proposed Standards: Staffing Requirements

FTE Students	Administrators Minimum and Excellent	Other Professionals		Technicians		Other Staff [a]		Total Staff	
		Minimum	Excellent	Minimum	Excellent	Minimum	Excellent	Minimum	Excellent
Under 200	1	.5	2	1	2	1	2	3.5	7
200–1,000	1	2	4	2	4	2	3	7	12
1,000–3,000	1	3	5	3	6	3	6	10	18
3,000–5,000	1	5	7	5	8	4	8	15	24
5,000–7,000	1	7	9	7	12	6	11	21	33
7,000–9,000	1	8	11	9	17	7	14	25	43
9,000–11,000	1	10	15	11	20	9	17	31	53
11,000–13,000	2	14	21	13	24	11	20	40	67
13,000–15,000	2	16	24	16	28	13	24	47	78
15,000–17,000	2	18	27	19	32	16	28	55	89
17,000–19,000	2	20	30	21	36	18	32	61	100

[a] Secretaries, clerks, door attendants, lab aides.

Learning center
Microcomputer lab
Tutoring center
Media production

Telecourse production
Instructional development
Printing services
Bookstore

Surprisingly, centralized library services are offered by only 95 percent and library user instruction by only 82.5 percent of respondents. Only 35 percent offer remedial assistance, while 33 percent provide microcomputer labs, and 27 percent offer instructional design services for faculty. Almost 18 percent do not offer bibliographic instruction (see Table 2).

Collections. Size of book collections ranges from 1,000 to 272,000 volumes. Over 40 percent of the LRC collections contain fewer than 30,000 volumes, the minimum requirement in the standards, which also stipulate that 50,000 volumes constitute an excellent collection for colleges with enrollments of three thousand or fewer students. Only 33 of the 146 colleges with such enrollments meet minimal standards, while 27 fall into the "excellent" category. Proposed standards for colleges of this size raise the minimum basic collection to 40,000 volumes and the excellent one to 60,000. Only nine responding colleges have collections meeting this new standard for excellence. Proposed standards for colleges with 9,000 or more FTEs set a 95,000-volume collection as minimal and one of 136,000 volumes as excellent (see Table 3). Of the responding institutions in this category, two meet the "minimum" and one meets the "excellent" requirements. Of the twelve colleges with enrollments of 12,000 or more, three fail to meet the basic collection standard of 125,000, seven meet that criterion, and two achieve excellence, reporting collections of over 200,000 volumes.

While larger institutions seem to comply more successfully with the proposed standards, one must keep in mind that many of them are multi-campus schools. Many meager collections reflect the very specialized ori-

Table 2. LRC Services

FTE	Number of Learning Centers	Number of Tutoring Centers	Number of Microlabs	Number of Instructional Design Labs
Under 1,000	25	17	25	10
1,000–3,000	43	22	38	35
3,000–5,000	22	19	19	25
5,000–7,000	12	5	14	8
7,000–8,000	3	3	2	0
8,000–9,000	3	1	3	3
9,000–10,000	2	3	3	3
10,000–11,000	3	2	3	2
11,000–12,000	2	0	2	2
12,000 or more	13	7	11	3
	128	79	120	98

Table 3. Proposed Standards: Collection Size

Basic Collection

FTE	Print Items	Serials	Video/Film	Other	Total
Under 200	20,000	200	30	1,200	21,430
200–1,000	30,000	230	45	1,500	31,775
1,000–3,000	40,000	300	125	2,100	42,525
3,000–5,000	60,000	500	400	3,000	63,900
5,000–7,000	80,000	700	700	3,600	85,000
7,000–9,000	95,000	850	750	4,000	101,600
9,000–11,000	110,000	900	800	4,800	116,700
11,000–13,000	125,000	1,000	850	5,400	132,250
13,000–15,000	140,000	1,200	900	5,800	147,800
15,000–17,000	155,000	1,500	950	6,000	163,450
17,000–19,000	170,000	1,800	1,000	6,500	179,300

Excellent Condition

FTE	Print Items	Serials	Video/Film	Other	Total
Under 200	30,000	350	125	3,000	33,475
200–1,000	45,000	400	140	3,600	49,140
1,000–3,000	60,000	600	400	4,800	65,800
3,000–5,000	85,000	800	750	6,600	93,150
5,000–7,000	112,000	1,000	1,250	11,000	125,250
7,000–9,000	136,000	1,200	1,600	13,000	151,800
9,000–11,000	166,000	1,400	1,800	15,000	184,200
11,000–13,000	200,000	1,600	2,000	18,000	221,600
13,000–15,000	240,000	1,800	2,200	21,000	265,000
15,000–17,000	285,000	2,100	2,400	24,000	313,500
17,000–19,000	320,000	2,400	2,600	27,000	352,000

entations of the institutions or are augmented by institutional resource sharing; nevertheless, most LRC print collections are clearly inadequate.

Ideally, LRC professionals and college administrators should find additional resources to upgrade their collections and services. The proposed standards recommend, as a minimum budget, 5 percent of the college's educational/general expenditures, and 9 percent to reach an excellent level of funding.

BI Programs in Community Colleges. Of the 366 responding institutions, only 302 (82.5 percent) indicate that they have bibliographic instruction programs. Most of these programs are integrated into freshman English courses, but some have been designed in response to requests by faculty members for specific classes, usually in business, nursing, speech, and vocational education but surprisingly seldom in history or the social sciences. This may suggest that history and social science instructors are not assigning research papers or requiring their students to become familiar with the professional literature in their fields.

Library Instruction for Remedial Programs. Community college administrators and LRC directors alike are aware that college enrollments have shifted dramatically to part-time, less well prepared, and more immediately career-oriented students, increasing the need for remedial work. Remedial library instruction gives every indication of being more expensive to offer than ordinary BI, since it is labor-intensive and involves using (and perhaps preparing) special materials, including bilingual ones. Yet there are relatively few campuses where the LRC and the learning centers are working together to address this need. The survey shows that only 34.6 percent of the LRCs contain learning centers, and fewer still (21.6 percent) have tutoring centers. Indeed, there seems to have been little change, according to results reported in a 1983-84 survey of a group of Texas community college libraries, which showed that developmental students are least likely to receive library skills instruction (Sisco, 1984).

This deficiency is also noted by Hisle (1988), who recommends that responsibility for such instructional services, perhaps shared with other college departments, be considered integral to the basic LRC mission. In general, this concept is supported in the proposed standards, which call for LRCs to provide services that support and expand instructional capabilities. Faced with increasing numbers of underprepared students and continuously evolving technological developments, LRC directors and deans must use the standards to mobilize support for adequate funding and staffing to expand or initiate important services, such as library literacy, to keep the LRC in the mainstream of campus instructional activities.

Course-Integrated and Academic-Support Instruction. Retention of students is a key issue in higher education today. Evidence exists that there has been a substantial decline in the proportion of community college students going on to four-year institutions (Eaton, 1988). Administrators are looking at success rates and becoming aware that students, especially minority students, need a support system for success. An LRC user education program can provide an important link in such a support system. Nearly half of the survey respondents (145, or 45 percent) indicate that their user education programs serve students intending to matriculate. Some also provide students with college survival skills, tutoring, and remedial instruction. All these labor-intensive activities require adequate staffing, funding, and the support of teaching faculty.

While 259 (70.8 percent) reported that their BI programs are "course-integrated," some seem to have interpreted the survey question loosely. Some librarians are indeed working closely with teaching faculty, but others interpret any specific request from a classroom instructor for bibliographic instruction as "course-integrated instruction." Tables 4 and 5 show the types of library instruction and success services that respondents offer.

Use of Computers in Bibliographic Instruction. Dubin and Kuhner (1985-86) identify the need to design computer programs to build analytical and critical-thinking skills, but the returns of the survey on which the article is based were too scattered to determine how broadly computers were being employed for user education. Fewer than 25 percent of those responding to the current survey use computers to develop library skills, even though the professional literature demonstrates that computers can be used effectively for interactive teaching, specialized library orientation, and other routine library instruction (see Table 6). Staff in only about 15

Table 4. Specific Group Instruction

	Number	Percentage
Developmental classes	93	36.90
Academic disciplines	215	85.32
Honors classes	38	15.08
ESL classes	45	17.86
Other	38	15.08

N = 249

Table 5. Success Services

	Number	Percentage
College survival skills	256	69.95
Peer tutoring	292	79.78
Remedial instruction	319	87.16
Honors instruction	138	37.70
Adult basic education	181	49.45
Academic alert system	92	25.14
Other (special counseling, tutoring)	34	9.29

Table 6. Computer Instruction

	Number	Percentage
Location of resources	42	46.15
Catalogue use	52	57.14
Index use	55	60.44
Search strategy	49	53.45
Other	22	24.18
N = 85		

percent of the LRCs responding to the questionnaire use computers in teaching search strategies. Unfortunately, the survey did not elicit information on how they are accomplishing this.

Evaluation of Bibliographic Instruction Programs. While LRCs have long been urged to evaluate their BI programs, only 211, or 58 percent, of survey respondents do so (see Table 7). Many think of BI evaluation in terms of elaborately constructed research projects using a variety of statistical measures, such as chi square and t tests. More fundamental than the techniques employed, however, are the measures by which success is judged. BI programs should be designed not merely to help students find materials or search for information but also to contribute to the learning processes that students use in these activities.

Whatever method librarians use, they must set standards not only to be accountable but also to measure improvement in users' skills. It is widely recognized that the professional standards are for "inputs" to library services and instruction, but, as Kania (1988) notes, LRCs also need "output" standards, to judge the end products of BI programs. The current survey reveals that 53 percent of respondents favor the development of such output performance standards.

Training for Bibliographic Instruction. Most librarians providing bibliographic instruction learn either on the job or by attending inservice and professional seminars and workshops and keeping up with the professional literature. Some create peer groups in their LRCs for role playing and experimentation. Respondents who mention their M.L.S. degrees as qualification for teaching library skills cite no specific graduate courses that helped prepare them.

Table 7. Evaluation of BI Programs

	Number	Percentage
Student questionnaire	124	58.77
Pre-post testing	44	20.85
Graded library assignment	97	35.97
Feedback from classroom instructor	143	67.77
Other	20	9.48

Many community college library administrators and professionals do not have the M.L.S. degree. Indeed, if the respondents are correct about the importance of the M.L.S. degree as a qualification for providing bibliographic instruction, perhaps the proposed standards should reflect that. The proposed standards (1989, p. 7) recommend that "the professional staff shall have a graduate degree from an accredited institution" and that the "training and experience of the chief administrator shall be as a librarian, a media specialist, or an information specialist, with cross-training desirable."

With rapid changes in the methods of accessing information and the growing need for remedial work on campuses, the profession may have to look more closely at credentialing. Perhaps graduate courses in bibliographic instruction should be mandatory in M.L.S. programs and for training those who lack the M.L.S. degree.

Current Realities and the Need for Change

At the height of the expansion of community colleges, in the mid 1960s, LRCs were at the cutting edge of technology. Imaginative administrators integrated print and nonprint collections and experimented with technology to deliver closed-circuit TV, provide instructional design services, produce TV programming, and institute telecourse instruction and delivery. They created an environment for a holistic library and obtained resources and respect across their campuses.

Something has happened to LRCs since that time. Most are no longer receiving the resources required to develop multimedia collections to meet current and future needs. Collections are inadequate, and staffs are too thin to meet the needs of students, particularly large numbers of nontraditional students. While these shortcomings may partially reflect financial constraints imposed by the taxpaying public, they may also reflect a loss of vision—either professional burnout, resulting from repeated failure to acquire necessary support, or professional complacency.

To regain a leadership role in the profession, LRC staff must revitalize their user education programs, not only by acquiring additional resources, enhancing their collections, bolstering their staffs, and acquiring inventories of data bases and computers but also by rethinking the ways in which they are delivering and evaluating bibliographic instruction. BI librarians may find it useful to explore the literature on learning styles, as discussed by Bodi (1990, p. 119), who observes that "meeting the various learning modes of students may be the key to improving teaching effectiveness." They must find ways to develop truly course-integrated BI, in partnership with teaching faculty, and to evaluate that instruction with performance standards that measure whether students have become independent library users.

Community college librarians will also have to manage an ever changing, complex, computer-centered communications system. In a state-of-the-art LRC, computer-driven programs of instruction will link the library to the classroom. Librarians will provide basic reference services by helping patrons use remote terminals. Library instruction will take on a new dimension as electronic reference services become the norm. Librarians will link researchers to systems and provide cohesiveness and direction in introducing new technologies (Caren, 1989). Methods of accessing and utilizing information will change and have a direct impact on user education.

Now that a course has been charted for two-year colleges in the 1990s, their LRCs should take a proactive stance regarding their role in instruction, a role that should include helping underprepared, first-generation college students and creating an environment that stresses academic achievement.

References

American Association of Community and Junior Colleges. *Building Communities: A Vision for a New Century.* Washington, D.C.: Association of Community and Junior Colleges, 1988. 58 pp. (ED 293 578)

Bodi, S. "Critical Thinking and Bibliographic Instruction: The Relationship." *Journal of Academic Librarianship,* 1988, *14* (3), 150–153.

Bodi, S. "Teaching Effectiveness and Bibliographic Instruction: The Relevance of Learning Styles." *College & Research Libraries,* 1990, *5* (2), 113–119.

Breivik, P. S. "Making the Most of Libraries." *Change,* 1987, *19* (4), 45–52.

Caren, L. "New Bibliographic Instruction for New Technology: Library Connections Seminar at the Rochester Institute of Technology." *Library Trends,* 1989, *37* (13), 366–373.

Dale, D. C. "The Learning Resources Center's Role in the Community College System." *College & Research Libraries,* 1988, *49* (3), 232–238.

Dubin, E., and Bigelow, L. "Community College Learning Resources Centers at the Crossroads: Illinois, A Case Study." *College & Research Libraries,* 1986, *47* (6), 596–603.

Dubin, E., and Kuhner, R. "Use of Microcomputers in Library Instruction." *Resource Sharing and Information Networks,* 1985-86, *3* (1), 65–82.

Eaton, J. S. *Colleges of Choice: The Enabling Impact of the Community College.* New York: American Council on Education, 1988.

Fjallbrant, N., and Malley, J. *User Education in Libraries.* (2nd ed.) London: Clive Bingley, 1984.

Hisle, W. L., Jr. "The Role of Learning Resources Services in Selected Community Colleges." Unpublished doctoral dissertation, University of Texas at Austin, 1988.

Kania, A. M. "Academic Library Standards and Performance Measures." *College & Research Libraries,* 1988, *49* (1), 16–23.

Kerr, T. J. "California's Community College Chief Looks to the '90s." *School and College,* 1988, *27* (3), 14–16.

Kreider, P. E., and Walleri, R. D. "Seizing the Agenda: Institutional Effectiveness and Student Outcomes for Community Colleges." *Community College Review,* 1988, *16* (2), 44–50.

Martell, C., and Ware, J. D. "Hard Facts, Hard Work: Academic Libraries and *A Nation at Risk*—A Symposium." *Journal of Academic Librarianship,* 1988, *14* (2), 72–81.

Sisco, P. A. "Bibliographic Instruction in Community Colleges." *New Jersey Libraries,* 1984, *17* (3), 7–14.

"Standards for Two-Year College Learning Resources Programs: A Draft." *College & Research Libraries News,* 1989, *50* (6), 496–505.

Svinicki, M., and Schwartz, B. A. *Designing Instruction for Library Users.* New York: Marcel Dekker, 1988.

Veit, F. *The Community College Library.* Westport, Conn.: Greenwood Press, 1975.

Young, P. H. "Library Research in the Future: A Prognostication." *College & Research Libraries News,* 1989, *50* (1), 7–10.

Eileen Dubin is assistant director for public services and collection management, Case Western Reserve University Libraries. She is past chair of the Community and Junior College Libraries Section of the Association of College and Research Libraries.

Examples of LRC involvement in teaching and learning are provided.

The Instructional Role of Two-Year College LRCs

Lisa Raufman, Dana Nicole Williams, Anita Colby

As the previous chapters have demonstrated, learning resources centers (LRCs) at community colleges are approaching their instructional responsibilities in a variety of ways. Most LRCs offer some form of library orientation, and all target their collection-development policies to support their colleges' instructional programs. Over the past ten years, many LRCs have increased their computer resources and become active partners in audiovisual services, computer-assisted instruction, and computer literacy programs. For example, in Platte's (1988) 1986 survey of the status of libraries and LRCs at Michigan's community colleges, all of the twenty-nine responding LRCs provided traditional reference, research, and bibliographic support to students and faculty; fifteen reported involvement in the production of audio, video, graphics, and photographic instructional resources; six provided learning-lab instruction, and six offered tutorial services; twenty-three circulated books to the community; and two-thirds were involved in some form of television-supported instruction. This chapter reviews recent documents and journal articles in the ERIC data base that highlight examples of LRCs' involvement in teaching and learning.

Bibliographic Instruction

Community colleges have needs for bibliographic instruction that are different from those of four-year colleges. Students at two-year colleges are not usually required to conduct in-depth research. Most study subjects at introductory rather than advanced levels, and, as commuters, most do not spend a great deal of time on campus outside of class (Yee, 1982). As a

NEW DIRECTIONS FOR COMMUNITY COLLEGES, no. 71, Fall 1990 © Jossey-Bass Inc., Publishers

group, these students exhibit widely varying levels of language and academic skills. All of these factors are important considerations in the development of programs for library instruction.

The methods employed by two-year colleges to deliver library instruction range from formal, for-credit courses to course-integrated library skills modules to self-paced individualized instruction. Janney's (1986) survey of the LRCs in North Carolina's community colleges revealed that the most prevalent approach to teaching library skills was the orientation tour, followed by individualized instruction and reference service. Seven colleges also required some students to take a bibliographic instruction course, and five others offered a library skills elective.

Miami–Dade Community College's South campus has developed a self-instructional library skills program that uses a two-part manual to provide information on the book-classification system, the card catalogue, major types of reference books, periodical indexes, and vertical files (Wine, 1983). In addition, the manual contains review exercises, in-library assignments, and computer-scored tests. The library skills program has been integrated into half of the college's English composition courses and has received favorable responses from instructors as well as from students.

Recognizing that the skill deficiencies of remedial students are a major obstacle to their effective use of the library, the LRC at Kingsborough Community College (New York) has developed a one-hour, hands-on library skills unit as part of the English Skills Lab program (Schneider and Fuhr, 1982). An in-class lecture and demonstration by a librarian is reinforced with a worksheet on the use of the catalogue and periodical indexes.

Glendale Community College (Arizona) also recently enhanced its bibliographic instruction program. A fifty-minute slide-tape and lecture orientation to the library has been integrated into basic writing courses. As a follow-up, students are required to complete an in-library exercise developed by the college's librarians. Librarians grade assignments and return them to English faculty members for incorporation into students' final grades (Williams and Miller, 1986).

Other Instructional Roles

LRCs are currently involved in providing instruction in a variety of subject areas and formats. The most common subjects taught in the LRC tend to be basic skills and library use. At certain colleges, however, vocational instruction, college survival skills, and computer literacy fall within the purview of the LRC.

Developmental Education. Holleman (1982) found that twelve of thirty LRCs provided remedial instruction through library-based learning laboratories. Similarly, a statewide survey in Texas revealed that 12.2 percent of learning centers' developmental education programs were administered by libraries (Rippey and Truett, 1983-84).

The experience of West Hills College (California) indicates that such library-based remedial programs can be very effective (Gerhardt, 1985-86). At West Hills, faculty develop the instructional approaches, an oversight committee determines policy, and the library director administers and evaluates the program. Classes are taught by humanities instructors on a rotating basis, and instructional support is provided by a staff of LRC assistants and paid tutors.

At Miami–Dade Community College's North campus, every student enrolled in remedial reading or writing is required to take the library-based Information Skills Lab (Suarez, 1985). The lab offers students instruction in the use of the library; college survival skills, such as reading Miami–Dade's computer-generated progress reports and planning a program of study; thinking skills, such as paying attention, remembering, and preparing for tests; and development of the personal skills and attitudes necessary to academic success.

Chattanooga State Technical Community College (Tennessee) has discovered a number of ways in which close relationships between developmental education instructors and college librarians can foster student learning (Houck, 1988). Librarians teach research skills to students in developmental English and study-skills courses, emphasizing the topics assigned in class. For developmental reading courses, librarians compile information on assigned topics and teach students to differentiate between primary and secondary sources. Developmental courses have participated increasingly in this program over the past five years.

Subject-Oriented Instruction. In cooperation with the Office Occupations Department at Laramie County Community College, the LRC developed a six-hour unit to explore the use of the library by secretaries (Donovan and Elliott, 1989). Students get hands-on experience with library resources that are also basic office and secretarial tools. They also visit state and public libraries.

Computer Literacy. The use of computers has increased tremendously in community colleges over the past decade, and many LRCs have become involved in computer-assisted instruction, self-paced computer laboratories, and computer literacy instruction.

The Lima Campus Library of the Ohio State University was selected as the location for the college's computer literacy program because its flexible hours were adaptable to the schedules of students and the general public (Hanson, 1984). Rather than serving as consultants or support staff, library staff members are actively involved as instructors in public training sessions designed to familiarize students and community members with the basics of computer operations, hardware, and software.

The New Mexico Military Institute's Toles Learning Center has over eighty terminals in its facility (McLaren, 1987). These offer students and faculty alike an opportunity to increase their computer literacy, with LRC staff guiding their independent progress. Students enrolled in formal computer courses, taught by faculty, share the Toles Learning Center with self-paced students.

Computer-Assisted Instruction. During the 1970s, several LRCs became involved in providing computer-assisted instruction (CAI). The National Science Foundation sponsored a number of these early projects, referred to as Time-Shared Computer-Controlled Information Television (TICCIT) programs (Terwilliger, 1985). TICCIT currently provides complete courses in algebra, English grammar, and remedial English, as well as supplementary instruction in other subject areas. In addition, learner control, student tracking, monitoring, and progress reports are built in.

A recent survey revealed that six libraries and LRCs at Michigan community colleges also provide learning-laboratory instruction for developmental and traditional courses (Platte, 1988). LRC staff members supervise these labs, working in conjunction with humanities and science instructors.

Telecourses. The LRC's role in the provision of telecourses varies greatly by campus. Many LRCs house videotapes of telecourse programs, as well as VCRs and monitors, so that students can watch programs they missed or review programs for exams. In Allen's (1982) discussion of the ways in which the LRC can use television and video technologies more effectively to support independent study, the LRC is considered to be in an excellent position to distribute cassettes and administer tests.

Bell (1986, p. 12) indicates that in most North Carolina community and technical colleges LRC personnel have acted "as local coordinators, liaisons, managers, and/or promoters of telecourses, teleprograms, and teleconferences." LRCs are also heavily involved in the dissemination of information about telecourses, the design and production of brochures, and interaction with the Center for Public Television.

Kirkwood Community College has an extensive telecourse service, run by the Kirkwood Telecommunications Center (KTC), a division of the LRC (Schmidt, 1987). This microwave system links classroom instruction with seven outlying campuses. KTC offers recertification courses in nursing, cosmetology, real estate, and insurance, as well as a number of community education courses.

Instructional Support and Development. Roark's (1983) model of integrated learning resources assigns the library an active role in the improvement of instruction. He argues that the involvement of librarians in curriculum planning and the participation of instructional staff in collection development provide a necessary bridge between the instructional program of a college and its library.

Major (1987) recommends that LRCs creating instructional development programs should consider the time constraints of faculty, address all levels of instructors' developmental needs, and involve other faculty in the development of materials for their peers.

The library at Jackson Community College (Michigan) houses an instructional development center (Major, 1987). Instructors can visit the center any time to use modules on specific instructional methods and strategies. Library-based instructional developers collaborate with instructors to produce these modules and the menu-driven system used to access them.

In Richland College's library, the Division of Instructional Development Services provides assistance with review, revision, and development of lessons, units, courses, and programs (Schmidt, 1987). In addition, by administering the college's Instructional Development Grant program, the division also helps instructors with test construction, evaluation, and research.

The library at Miami–Dade Community College's North campus offers three workshops to assist faculty members in the development of library assignments (Suarez, 1985): "Basic Instruction in Services and Resources Available at the North Campus Library," "Practical Application," and "The Mechanics of Library Assignments." At Miami–Dade's South campus, the library supports instruction in several other ways (Watters, 1986). Librarians offer in-class lectures on library use, prepare bibliographies, and conduct on-line computer searches on topics related to developmental and gifted instruction. The library maintains a special collection of materials to help students prepare for the College-Level Academic Skills Test. Librarians have also prepared fifty-two reading lists in various disciplines, to encourage students to read, and they serve as mentors to minority and honors students.

Conclusion

The community college LRC is expected to provide a range and diversity of programs and services beyond that of any other library. The "Guidelines for Two-Year College Learning Resources Programs" (1972) establish a role for community college libraries in both academic instruction and instructional development. These guidelines, reaffirmed in 1982, call for community college librarians to be involved in teaching and to work with administrators and staff to design, implement, and evaluate instructional and educational systems.

The LRC's ability to fulfill its current mission and future roles will depend on many factors, some within and some beyond the control of the LRC itself. Terwilliger (1985) identifies some of the external forces as advances in computer and communications technology, changes in the makeup and needs of community colleges' student bodies, and the financial base of the colleges as a whole. Internal factors include the structure of the

LRC and the LRC's perceived value in the college, as well as the professional competence and continuing education of LRC staff. In her assessment of the future of the LRC, Terwilliger (1985, p. 538) concludes that "the LRC is the campus unit which can fuse the instruments of technology and the accumulated knowledge of the past, present, and future."

References

Allen, K. W. "The Utilization of Telecourses in the Learning Resources Center." *Community & Junior College Libraries*, 1982, *1* (1), 11–20.

Bell, M. B. "An Opportunity and a Challenge." *North Carolina Libraries*, 1986, *44* (1), 10–12. (ED 271 132)

Donovan, S., and Elliott, M. "Profile of a Community College LRC: Laramie Community College." *Community & Junior College Libraries*, 1989, *6* (2), 71–74.

Gerhardt, S. L. "Library-Administered Remediation: One Program That Works." *Community & Junior College Libraries*, 1985–86, *4* (2), 41–44.

"Guidelines for Two-Year College Learning Resources Programs." *College & Research Libraries News*, 1972, *33*, 305–314.

Hanson, C. "Computer Literacy in an Academic Library: Technological Hit or Myth." *Community & Junior College Libraries*, 1984, *3* (1), 3–11.

Holleman, P. "How Widely Has the Learning Resources Program Concept Been Adopted?" *Community & Junior College Libraries*, 1982, *1* (1), 6–10.

Houck, T. "Library Skills Instruction for Developmental Courses." *Community & Junior College Libraries*, 1988, *5* (2), 53–56.

Janney, S. "Bibliographic Instruction at Learning Resources Centers in North Carolina." *North Carolina Libraries*, 1986, *44* (1), 16–22. (ED 271 132)

McLaren, B. M. "Profile of New Mexico Military Institute's Toles Learning Center: Marketing the LRC into the Twentieth Century." *Community & Junior College Libraries*, 1987, *5* (1), 31–42.

Major, H. T. "User-Oriented Instructional Development: An Opportunity for Community College Libraries." *Community & Junior College Libraries*, 1987, *5* (1), 19–30.

Platte, J. P. (ed.). *The Status and Prospects of Library/Learning Resource Centers at Michigan Community Colleges*. Lansing: Michigan Community College Association, 1988. 103 pp. (ED 306 979)

Rippey, D. T., and Truett, C. "The Developmental Student and the Community College Library." *Community College Review*, 1983–84, *11* (3), 41–47.

Roark, D. B. "Reorganizing Toward Instructional Development." *Community & Junior College Libraries*, 1983, *1* (4), 39–48.

Schmidt, W. D. *Learning Resources Programs That Make a Difference: A Source of Ideas and Models from Exemplary Programs in the Field*. Washington, D.C.: Association for Educational Communications and Technology, 1987. 124 pp. (ED 283 511)

Schneider, A., and Fuhr, M. L. "The Library's Role in Remediation: A Cooperative Program of Physical and Philosophical Integration at Kingsborough Community College." *Community & Junior College Libraries*, 1982, *1* (2), 47–58.

Suarez, C. C. "The Library and Remedial/Developmental/Compensatory Education: A Case Study." *Library Trends*, 1985, *33* (4), 487–499.

Terwilliger, G. "Forecasting the Future of Community College Learning Resources Centers." *Library Trends*, 1985, *33* (4), 523–539.

Watters, R. D. "A Climate for Excellence: Paving the Way for Student Success at Miami-Dade South's Library." *Community & Junior College Libraries*, 1986, *4* (4), 7–27.

Williams, J. J., and Miller, L. A. "Glendale Community College Instructional Materials Center: A Model for Student Success." *Community & Junior College Libraries,* 1986, 4 (4), 29–33.

Wine, E. "The Library Instruction Program at Miami-Dade South." *Community & Junior College Libraries,* 1983, 2 (2), 57–63.

Yee, S. G. "Library Instruction in the Community College Setting." *Community & Junior College Libraries,* 1982, 1 (1), 53–56.

Lisa Raufman and Dana Nicole Williams are students at the University of California at Los Angeles.

Anita Colby is associate director of the ERIC Clearinghouse for Junior Colleges.

INDEX

OTHER TITLES AVAILABLE IN THE
NEW DIRECTIONS FOR COMMUNITY COLLEGES SERIES
Arthur M. Cohen, Editor-in-Chief
Florence B. Brawer, Associate Editor